Urban Legends: The Collection

By

Cindy Parmiter

Introduction

Chapter 1:   Spring-Heeled Jack
Chapter 2:   The Hollow-Eyed Girl
Chapter 3:   The Phantom Hitchhiker
Chapter 4:   Highway Terror
Chapter 5:   A Babysitter's Worst Nightmare
Chapter 6:   Killer Clowns
Chapter 7:   Bloody Mary
Chapter 8:   The Killer in the Backseat
Chapter 9:   Alligators in the Sewer
Chapter 10: The Mole People
Chapter 11: The Earwig
Chapter 12: The Rat King
Chapter 13: The Boogeyman
Chapter 14: The Stolen Kidney
Chapter 15: The Haunted Painting
Chapter 16: The Red Spot
Chapter 17: The Dog Boy
Chapter 18: Watch at Your Own Risk
Chapter 19: Black Dogs
Chapter 20: The Show Must Go On
Chapter 21: Little Green Men
Chapter 22: 100 Steps Cemetery
Chapter 23: The Bunny Man
Chapter 24: Hider in the House
Chapter 25: Water Babies
Chapter 26: The Dark Watchers
Chapter 27: The Licker
Chapter 28: The Swamp Grunch
Chapter 29: The Alice Killings
Chapter 30: The Death Car
Chapter 31: The Ghosts of the Woods
Chapter 32: Zombie Road
Chapter 33: The Elevator Man

Chapter 34: Tanning Bed Terror
Chapter 35: Slaughterhouse Canyon
Chapter 36: The Open Grave
Chapter 37: Mandy
Chapter 38: Nain Rouge
Chapter 39: The Roommate
Chapter 40: Love Rollercoaster
Chapter 41: The Hamburger Man
Chapter 42: Shtriga

Acknowledgements
Resources
Films and Television Related to These Stories
Publishing/Copyright

Introduction

Urban legends are stories—some well-known, some obscure—
that usually start off with a grain of truth. Over time, many
develop into tall tales that bear little resemblance to the original
events. Stories tend to take on a life of their own as they pass
from one person to another, and urban legends are no
exception. Ultimately, it becomes difficult to determine what
part of the story is true and what has been exaggerated.

This book contains the combined volumes of my previous
offerings on the subject: *Could It Be True: Urban Legends* and
Spooky Urban Legends & the Stories Behind Them. To spice
things up a bit, three intriguing new tales have been added to
the mix.

Included in these pages are accounts of a demonic presence
that terrorized Great Britain in the 19th century, reptiles
rumored to inhabit the sewers of New York City, brain-eating
insects, killer clowns, a real-life boogeyman, a babysitter's
unspeakable night of terror, vanishing hitchhikers, a cursed
automobile, sinister entities that stalk the night, a possessed
doll, alien visitations, haunted cemeteries, predators who
preferred human game, mythical creatures and much, much
more.

Now that the formalities are out of the way, the time has come
to delve into the world of urban legends, a place where nothing
is ever as it seems.

Chapter 1:
Spring-Heeled Jack

The strange phenomenon that became known as "Spring-Heeled Jack" began in Great Britain around 1837 and would last for sixty-seven years before finally coming to an end. Who, or what, was Spring-Heeled Jack? No one knows for sure, but theories abound. Was he a demon sent from Hell or simply a man who could turn from being an English gentleman into a terrifying monster in the blink of an eye? You be the judge.

It all began with a young girl who claimed that, as she was walking home from her job late one evening, she was accosted by a creature with bone-chillingly cold hands as she cut through a back alley. He towered over her and his eyes glowed like fire. He lashed out at the girl with his claws, which were as sharp as knives. Her terrified screams frightened away her otherworldly assailant before he could do any permanent damage.

The girl reported the attack to authorities and a manhunt ensued. No sign of the man she described could be found. One day later, he struck again just a few blocks from where the attack on the girl had taken place.

This time, the attack occurred in the daylight. The driver of a street carriage reported that, as he was navigating along a back street, a man suddenly leaped out in front of his coach. The driver had to swerve to avoid hitting the man which caused the carriage to crash, critically injuring the driver.

The tall, thin figure who had caused the accident escaped unharmed. Witnesses at the scene told investigators that he had seemed quite happy with the havoc he had created. The man, if it was a man, had thrown his head back and laughed at his handy work. He then turned and jumped over a barrier said to be at least nine feet high. The crowd that had gathered could still hear his ear-splitting cackle as he disappeared from sight.

After the latest incident, reports of a man, usually dressed in a black cloak who would accost people in dark alleys, began to flood police agencies all over the country. He was turning up everywhere, sometimes in two places at once. His favorite targets seemed to be women who he found walking alone. Whether it be day or night, he didn't seem to care. Whoever this predator was, he had little fear of being seen.

More often than not, the attacker would be frightened away by the victim's screams. What made this rogue different from any other was that he didn't just walk away or even run, it was that he would escape by leaping over houses and onto rooftops, laughing all the while.

As time passed, sightings increased. Police agencies all across Britain continued receiving complaints from citizens regarding this strange man who seemed to be showing up more and more often. Victims and witnesses alike came forward and gave descriptions of the assailant.

The man was described as being very tall and thin. Some witnesses said that he looked very much like any other man and that he spoke with a proper English accent. Others, however, had seen him as something far more frightening.

Some of those unlucky souls who had encountered the stranger said that he had the appearance of a devil with blazing red eyes and horns sprouting from his forehead. His hands were skeletal with long sharp claws like talons. They would say that to meet up with him was to see evil incarnate.

There were times when this mystery man could be heard, but not seen. Families would be in their homes, safe and sound, when their peace would be disrupted by the clatter of something above their heads. It sounded as though someone was running, or leaping, across their rooftops. The noises weren't like anything they had heard before. And, whatever was up there wasn't human. Whatever it was had hooves instead of feet.

It was after the attack on the coachman that London newspapers gave the anonymous attacker a name: "Spring-Heeled Jack" for his penchant for leaping over high buildings and fences to escape capture.

As tends to happen when a story grips a nation, copycats began to emerge. Anytime a prank was pulled, it was attributed to Jack. If a house was burgled, a rock thrown through a window or a woman accosted; it had to be Jack up to his old tricks.

Fearful residents of cities and towns alike began looking over their shoulders lest Jack leap upon them and fix them with his icy claws. He was turning up everywhere. A gardener claimed that he had encountered Jack and that it wasn't a man at all, but an animal the size of a bear. Others claimed that Jack was the devil himself.

It was in 1838 that the search for this elusive enigma took on a new urgency. It began when a girl named Jane Alsop was lured out of her home by someone claiming to be a policeman. He had seemed like a gentleman and Jane had no reason to doubt that he was who he said he was.

The man told her that he had captured Spring-Heeled Jack just a little ways down the street from her house. He needed her to fetch a candle and come with him to take a look at the culprit.

The unfailingly obedient girl did as she was told. After retrieving a lit candle from her home, she followed the stranger outside into the darkness.

Once the man had lured Jane away from the safety of her family, he pounced. His demeanor and appearance drastically changed in an instant. The guise of the kindly policeman had been replaced by a terrifying creature with ghostly white skin and glowing red eyes.

No longer did the man speak in the voice of an English gentleman. Now, when he opened his mouth, he spewed forth flames instead of words. Jane had seen Jack's true face and she was horrified.

She tried to run back to her home nearby, but he grabbed at her with his talon-like fingers. He ripped at her clothes and tore at her flesh. Just as it seemed that all hope was lost, one of Jane's sisters heard the commotion outside and came to her aid. Never known to take on more than one victim at a time, Jack disappeared into the night, escaping not by running away, but by leaping high up onto the rooftops.

A massive police investigation ensued. Jane was clearly traumatized, both physically and emotionally. This Jack, whoever he was, had to be stopped before he could strike again, which as it happened, would be sooner than later.

One week after the brutal attack on Jane Alsop, Jack was back. This time it would be young Lucy Scales and her sister who would encounter the malicious stranger.

The girls had been returning from a visit with their brother when they were confronted by a man who was blocking the path they were walking on. As they attempted to pass by him, the man suddenly opened his mouth and blew fire into Lucy's face. He then leapt out of sight, cackling all the while.

Temporarily blinded, she dropped to the ground and covered her face with her hands. She immediately began to convulse as though in the grips of an epileptic seizure. Lucy had never before suffered a seizure and her sister was at a loss as to what to do. More frightening still, the fit wouldn't stop. All her sister could do was to stand by helplessly as she lay writhing on the pavement.

Lucy's brother, whose home the girls had just left, heard his sister screaming for help. He ran down the street and found Lucy, still lying on the ground in the throes of a violent seizure. His other sister was in shock and couldn't stop screaming. Finally, able to calm her down, the brother asked her to help him pick Lucy up and carry her home.

The family immediately filed a complaint with the local police department. Although they worked tirelessly on the case, no one was ever charged with the attack on Lucy. Several men were questioned, but nothing came of it and for good reason.

Several suspects in the crimes against both Lucy and Jane confessed to the misdeeds. Some even gave details that seemed to prove that they were telling the truth, but no charges were ever filed. Both girls were adamant that their assailant had breathed fire and they refused to back down. Since none of the suspects possessed that very unusual ability, the cases were thrown out.

Alleged sightings of Jack continued for years. He was even reported to be paying the occasional visit to Scotland to spread his mischief around a bit. Again, even though many witnesses reported seeing him, he could never be caught in the act by authorities.

News agencies began receiving letters from an anonymous source claiming that the antics of Spring-Heeled Jack had started with a dare. A man had been challenged by a group of friends to pull some pranks that would get everyone's attention. Things got out of hand when what were supposed to be harmless shenanigans turned into criminal activity.

As with most other tips that investigators received, the man who was named in the letter denied any wrongdoing and the matter was dropped for lack of evidence. The search continued for the elusive Jack.

Newspapers all over Britain still reported his exploits. Sometimes, Jack was just a normal-looking man who would attack unsuspecting drivers on the road. At other times he was a demon of unusual speed and strength who could call forth fire to silence his victims.

One of the most intriguing, and believable, encounters with Spring-Heeled Jack occurred on a warm summer night near the barracks of a military base known as Aldershot. In 1877, a sentry on night watch was surprised by a stranger who appeared out of the darkness and began swiftly approaching him on foot.

The soldier ordered the figure to halt, but the interloper paid him no mind. Instead, the tall cloaked figure walked right up to the sentry and proceeded to slap him repeatedly across the face.

Another guard who was on duty that night saw the attack and fired at the stranger he witnessed slapping his compatriot. As it turned out, either he had terrible aim or his target was invincible because the shots had no effect whatsoever. The cloaked figure simply turned and leaped high up onto the tops of the buildings as he made his escape.

The soldiers, who weren't easily spooked, couldn't explain what had happened that night. The barracks was on alert after the incident. They were told to shoot any unidentified persons on sight.

Since the cloaked stranger was never seen again at Aldershot, it has been speculated that he got wind of the orders and decided to make himself scarce.

Over time, the sightings of Jack became less and less frequent before eventually ceasing altogether. Perhaps Spring-Heeled Jack, whoever he was, died a natural death thereby ending his reign of terror.

If Jack was not a man, but a demon sent from someplace we dare not venture, maybe he returned to that dark underworld from which he came leaving us, these many years later, to still ponder his identity and hope that he is well and truly gone from this earth for good.

Chapter 2:
The Hollow-Eyed Girl

I first became aware of the story of the "Hollow-Eyed Girl" around Halloween 2015. A friend of mine on social media had related a bizarre experience she claimed occurred on her way home from work one evening.

It was just after dark when, while driving along a relatively deserted street, the woman had seen a young girl standing in the middle of the roadway. The child had long black hair and was wearing a lacy white dress. She looked to be no more than ten years old.

My friend stopped to offer assistance to the child who immediately ran up to the car and started demanding to be let in. The woman refused. She thought it strange that the child kept her face hidden with her hands as she spoke.

The woman asked the girl where her parents were. The child wouldn't answer. She just kept repeating the same thing over and over: "Take me with you."

The woman didn't know what to do. Feeling sorry for the child, she opened the car door and was about to let her come inside when the girl dropped her hands, revealing that she had no eyes. There were only deep, black hollows where the orbs should have been.

In a panic, she pushed the girl away and shut the car door which only served to infuriate her. Almost instantly, she began pounding on the side of the driver's door and screaming: "TAKE ME WITH YOU!"

Terrified, the woman sped away, the screaming girl running along behind her. Eventually, she lost sight of the child. She phoned authorities and told them of her encounter with the ghostly girl who had no eyes. To her surprise, the officer she spoke to informed her that they had been receiving calls about the girl all evening.

My friend's warning had been this: beware of a young girl with long black hair who may attempt to flag you down demanding a ride. Whatever you do, keep driving. This was not a child, but something evil that had taken the form of something familiar and nonthreatening.

The message was shared time and time again until someone finally let the cat out of the bag: the whole episode was a hoax. Ignore the post; there are no demon children out there trying to hijack unsuspecting motorists.

The whole thing got me thinking, so I did a little research and found that sightings of the Hollow-Eyed Girl, as she is known, have been reported since the early 1980s. It was in the Cannock Chase area of the United Kingdom that the first reported encounter took place. It wouldn't be long before similar stories found their way across the Atlantic and then worldwide.

The alleged encounters were all strikingly similar. Motorists, and sometimes pedestrians, would stop to help a child who was usually standing in the middle of the street. Sometimes the child, almost always a girl with long black hair, would be standing there silently. At other times, she would be screaming.

It was nearly impossible to get a good look at the child, at least at first. Her eyes were always obscured. Sometimes a hoodie was pulled down over her face. On other occasions, she would be wearing sunglasses or simply covering her face with her hands. Once the barrier came down and the eyes, or lack thereof, were revealed panic would ensue. Besides having black pits instead of eyes, the children were also said to have very white or bluish skin, much like that of a corpse.

Encounters with the children happened in both the daylight hours and late into the night. Although most accounts involve a lone child, there have been several occasions when people claim that groups of these terrifying ghostly children accosted them.

Usually, it is around Halloween when someone will answer a knock on their door. They open it and find a group of children, all with jet black hair and old-fashioned, frilly white clothing standing on the doorstep. The strangers all either have their heads down or are hiding their faces with their hands.

One of the children will speak up and ask, in a quiet voice, to come inside. When the homeowner questions why the child needs to come in, they receive no answer. The child will again ask to enter the home, only this time they will raise their voice. This continues until the child is shouting to be let in.

The frightened homeowner usually shuts the door and locks it at this point leaving the angry children to pound on the door and turn the doorknob in an attempt to gain entry. Police are called to the scene, but the children are long gone by the time they arrive. No trace of them is found and the incidents are filed away as Halloween pranks.

There have also been reports that the images of these children have been inadvertently caught on film. A mother who had taken her children on an outing to a park one day for a picnic had gathered them together for a family photo. She snapped the picture and thought nothing more of it. That is until later when she saw the developed photo.

When the woman received the pictures back from the chemist a few days later, she noticed something very odd about the picture she had taken that day in the park. There, standing behind her children, was the image of another child. This was definitely not a member of her family. This child had no eyes.

The woman was absolutely positive that the child had not been there when the picture was taken; she would surely have seen her. If the interloper had been present, she wasn't visible to the naked eye. She had, nonetheless, shown up on film.

So, who are the children with the white, ghostlike faces and hollow pits where their eyes should be? Since most sightings occur in streets, railway stations and subways, it has been speculated that they are the spirits of children who have perished on the tracks or in automobile accidents.

It is always possible that the sightings are the result of over active imaginations or mass hysteria. Even so, it is curious that the alleged encounters are strikingly similar, right down to the smallest details.

While some of the stories are undoubtedly fakes, others seem quite plausible. Perhaps, as many devotees believe, every good urban legend does indeed begin with at least a grain of truth.

Keeping this in mind, it could be that, somewhere just outside of our reality, the spirits of children taken long ago, still roam the land of the living in search of refuge. Maybe, every now and again, they cross over to this side in their quest for a home. If this is the case, they couldn't pick a better time of year than Halloween when ghouls and goblins and children with no eyes can walk among us and be accepted—that is, until their secrets are revealed.

Chapter 3:
The Phantom Hitchhiker

Along the same lines as the Hollow-Eyed Girl is the legend of the phantom, or disappearing, hitchhiker. It usually goes something like this:

A man is driving down a deserted street late one night when, out of nowhere, a beautiful girl steps out of the darkness and waves to him. He pulls the car over and the girl tells him that she needs a ride home. She lives just up the road. She is usually distraught, sometimes crying.

Unable to resist her pleas, the man tells her to get in. The two of them ride along quietly until the girl points to a house and asks to be dropped off. The man stops and lets her out of the car and then watches her walk toward the house.

The hitchhiker turns for one last look at the driver who was kind enough to give her a ride and then, just like that, she disappears into thin air right before his eyes. Shocked and unable to believe what he has just seen, the man gets out and looks for the girl. She is nowhere to be found.

Summoning his courage, the man approaches the house and knocks on the door. It is very late and all of the lights are off. After a few moments, an elderly woman answers the door. She looks a bit disturbed by the presence of this stranger on her front steps.

He apologizes for bothering her so late before telling her the story of the hitchhiker who had asked for a ride to her house. He goes on to describe the girl, right down to the clothes she was wearing. He then inquires if the girl made it safely inside.

The woman's face turns ashen. She begins to tear up as she explains that although the girl had lived there many years ago, he couldn't possibly have given her a ride on that night or any other.

She goes on to say that his description fits her daughter Abigail, who died on the road on that very night seventeen years earlier. Tragically, she had been walking home from a party when she was struck down by a hit and run driver.

The man would later learn that he wasn't the only one who had given Abigail a ride over the years. She was known to haunt the road that she had been killed on, always trying to find her way back home, but never making it inside. Each time she was dropped off at the house, she disappeared just before crossing the threshold.

That is just one version of the story, there are many variations, but they all have the same basic premise. Someone who died, usually in an automobile accident of some sort, is seen wandering the road where the tragedy occurred, usually on the anniversary of their death. They stop cars and ask for a ride home, only to disappear either on the way to their destination or once they get there.

For decades, people all over the world have claimed that they have given rides to hitchhikers who vanished into thin air. The phenomenon occurs in the United States, Europe and Asia alike. The stories are all remarkably similar to the one you just read.

For every person who says that they have had such an encounter, there is a skeptic who will tell you that it is not possible. People don't haunt the areas they died in, and even if they did, they wouldn't be stopping cars and asking for rides.

Theories abound regarding the stories of phantom hitchhikers and the motorists who claim to have offered them rides. Hallucinations are one explanation. After driving for long periods, especially at night, one could begin to see things that aren't there. Of course, that wouldn't explain why so many people have nearly identical experiences.

As with all urban legends, it could just be a hoax, perpetrated on a grand scale. One person hears it and then another, until it spreads all over the world. It begins with "This happened to a friend of a friend" and then takes off like a shot.

It could be that at least some of the stories in question really did happen, though they may have been elaborated on over the years. Maybe drivers did pick up hitchhikers only to lose sight of them in the darkness making it seem as though they vanished.

There is also the possibility, however remote, that some of the encounters with phantom hitchhikers did, indeed, occur. For those who believe in ghosts, it isn't out of the realm of possibility that a lost soul might be trapped in a purgatory where they are forced to relive the last night of their life over and over again until they reach a destination that no longer welcomes them, thereby keeping them in limbo for eternity.

Some will scoff at the notion, but life isn't always black and white and neither, to be sure, is the afterlife. Not everything can be explained, nor should it be.

Chapter 4:
Highway Terror

It was sometime in the early 1990s that my overprotective mother began cautioning me to never, ever flash my high beams at anyone I encountered on the road who had neglected to turn on their headlights. By committing this grave error, I would unwittingly be signing my death warrant. Apparently, she had heard somewhere that thoroughfares were hunting grounds for killers on the lookout for Good Samaritans to chase down and slaughter. The bottom line was this: mind your own business or suffer the consequences.

At the time, rumors were rampant that random psychopaths, and/or marauding gang members, were cruising with their headlights off, waiting with bated breath for someone to flash their high beams. When a passing driver would alert them to the problem, the killers would pounce.

Once the trap had snapped, the car full of homicidal maniacs would give chase and run the other motorist off the road. The well-intentioned driver, along with anyone else in the vehicle, would be subjected to any number of unspeakable acts before being systematically killed. The bodies would then be abandoned on the side of the road as the psychos drove off into the night in search of more victims. The motto of these thrill-killers seemed to be the apropos "No good deed goes unpunished."

As improbable as this scenario may sound, it is thought to have sprung from an actual event. It all began with the terrifying ordeal suffered by a secretary and her companion in Stockton, California in 1992.

The woman was a passenger in a car driven by her friend when they saw a car coming towards them in the darkness. The car didn't have its lights on so they motioned to whoever was driving to let them know that they needed to turn on the headlights.

Unfortunately for them, the driver of the oncoming car thought that the secretary and her friend were using obscene gestures and he and the other people in his car became enraged. One of them pulled out a gun and fired into the secretary's car. The woman, Kelly Freed, was killed instantly.

It turned out that the shooter was a teenager. He and his friends hadn't realized that their headlights had been off. They weren't gang members and it had not been a ploy of any kind. They were just hotheaded kids who let their tempers get the better of them, and an innocent woman lost her life as a result.

So, although bands of merciless killers traveling the roadways hoping that someone flashes them a warning so they can descend upon and slaughter them at their leisure is a stretch; it isn't beyond the realms of possibility. After all, there are plenty of people walking among us who are capable of violence with little provocation.

Not everyone sees things the same way and an innocent gesture can be mistaken for something else by someone with a hot temper or a fragile grip on reality. So, when I'm driving late at night and see a car coming towards me with its lights off, do I warn them? Um, nope, I keep on driving and hope for the best. Better safe than sorry.

Chapter 5:
A Babysitter's Worst Nightmare

Many of us grew up watching horror movies in which the
hapless babysitter was terrorized by a mysterious caller. The
police would try to trace the call, but it would end just before
they could pinpoint where it was coming from. Until, that last
call when the trace is finally successful and we find out that—
gasp—he was upstairs the whole time!

Anyone who ever spent an evening babysitting was wary of
any little sound after watching those films. Every floor creak or
window rattling was surely an intruder just waiting to strike.
Checking and rechecking to make sure the doors were locked
became second nature.

After all of that worry, things usually ended on a happy note.
The parents arrived home to find that everything was as it
should be. The children were tucked safely in their beds and
the babysitter made it home, unscathed, with a few dollars in
her pocket to boot.

So, where did the legend of the terrorized babysitter get its
start? The most likely place was in Columbia, Missouri in
1950. It was there that a thirteen-year-old girl, Janett
Christman, was asked by a family she had known for quite
some time to babysit while they spent a night out. It was a
chance for her to earn some spending money and the young girl
jumped at the opportunity.

No one knows when the nightmare for Janett actually started,
but it was around 10:30 that a frantic call was placed to the
local police department. An obviously distraught girl was on
the line. She was screaming that she needed help. "Come
quick" were her last words before the line went dead. She
hadn't given her name or location. All the officer on duty could

do was to wait and hope that she would call again. At that time, they didn't have the ability to trace a call that ended so abruptly.

The family who Janett was babysitting for arrived home well after midnight. They were puzzled to find that the front door had been left unlocked. They entered the house and were greeted by a grisly scene they would never forget.

The body of their teenage babysitter lay in a pool of blood on the living room floor. There were shards of glass in another area from a broken window that they assumed the killer had used to enter the home. It was later determined that the broken window had been a ruse to throw investigators off the trail. There were no signs, inside or out, that indicated that anyone had entered or exited through the window.

The police department was immediately called as the frantic parents rushed upstairs to check on their children. They were relieved to find them safe in their beds, blissfully unaware of what had taken place downstairs as they slept.

Investigators determined that Janett had been sexually assaulted before being strangled to death. She had also been bludgeoned about the head at some point during the attack.

The officers who examined the crime scene felt that the young victim had known her killer and that she had willingly allowed them to enter the home that night. They came to this conclusion after finding that there were no signs of a struggle. Strangely, both the front and back doors had been left unlocked. It was determined that whoever the killer was, he had staged the broken window to make it appear as though the attack had occurred during a break-in.

It wasn't long before police had a suspect. People who had known Janett said that they could think of only one person who might have wanted to do her harm. The man they named was a twenty-seven-year-old acquaintance of both her and the family she had been babysitting for. His name was Robert Mueller.

It was common knowledge among the people who knew them that Mueller had a crush on the young girl. She, however, did not return the sentiment. He was known to make crude comments about the teenager to anyone who would listen. Disturbingly, he seemed to fixate on her figure and how well-developed she was for her age.

Police were confident that they had their man, but Mueller surprised everyone by passing a lie detector test. Since there was no physical evidence linking him to the murder, he was never charged with any crime. The murder of Janett Christman remains unsolved to this day.

Was the killer someone she knew and let into the house that night? Did this person she trusted suddenly turn on her before she knew what was happening? Was Janett the terrified girl who had phoned police that night begging for help only to have the call cut short by her killer?

All of those things are probable, but it is also possible that a complete stranger attacked and murdered the teenager that night. It's possible that every babysitter's nightmare of being set upon by a stranger in the house had become Janett's reality.

Chapter 6:
Killer Clowns

Nothing stops some of us dead in our tracks like the mention of the dreaded "c" word: clown. I prefer the term demon spawn, but it's a matter of personal preference. Clowns can find a place in every nightmare, including a babysitter's, as you are about to see.

This legend begins with a babysitter who has already tucked her charges in bed for the night. She notices a large clown doll sitting in a chair in one of the bedrooms. Thoroughly put off, she shuts the door and goes back downstairs.

Later, when the sitter goes upstairs to check on the children, she sees that the doll has moved, it is now in a different room, propped up in a corner. Assuming that one of the kids has moved the doll, she closes the door and returns to the living room to watch some television.

A short time later, the children's father calls to make sure everything is all right and to tell the sitter that they will be home later than expected. After assuring him that all is well, she mentions, half-jokingly, that she is a little bit spooked by the life-size clown doll in the bedroom.

He finds her comment somewhat puzzling since the family doesn't own any such doll. Just then, the girl turns to face the stairs leading up to the bedrooms and there, standing before her, is a menacing clown holding a butcher knife. On the other end, the man hears a scream, followed by an unsettling silence, as the line goes dead.

Clowns are the stuff of nightmares, make no mistake about it. So, where and when did these human oddities with the painted on smiles and bulbous red noses have their beginnings?

The word clown, which at the time meant "boor or peasant," was first recorded in 1560. Clowns as we know them originated in the 1800s. An actor named Joseph Grimaldi began painting his face for stage performances and, voila, the clown was born.

Circus clowns began to appear around 1860 as a distraction for the audiences between acts. Initially intended to be comic relief, the lines became blurred over time and clowns, for some, became a source of fear. That can be blamed, in part, on the theory that the clown's painted on face can sometimes hide a sinister persona, like that of "Pogo," better known as the infamous serial killer John Wayne Gacy.

Gacy was said to have tortured and murdered at least thirty-three boys and men in Illinois in the 1970s. Besides being a soulless serial killer, he was also a husband, father, successful businessman and all around pillar of the community. In his spare time, he dressed as a clown and entertained children at hospitals and parties.

Fancying himself an artist; Gacy painted self-portraits of himself as "Pogo" while sitting on Illinois' death row. He was executed for his crimes on May 10, 1994. This was one case of a truly evil person who took on the clown persona to fool people into thinking he was something he wasn't: harmless.

Stories still crop up every now and again of misdeeds that are attributed to people dressed as clowns. In 2008, reports surfaced online of people in clown costumes roaming the streets of Chicago attempting to abduct children. The sinister clowns used balloons and trickery in their efforts to lure youngsters into windowless vans. Whether this actually happened or not is up for debate. Some people swear they saw the clowns, but no solid evidence exists that proves that it actually happened.

Clowns started out as hard-working entertainers and, for the most part, they remain just that today. There are many talented performers out there who do a wonderful job of making audiences laugh at their antics.

Not all clowns are bad or scary, but over time they have taken on a dark persona that many find disturbing. An aversion to clowns, or coulrophobia, is a very real phenomenon. For sufferers, the paralyzing fear of the scary clown trumps the harmless comedian every time.

Chapter 7:
Bloody Mary

A group of people get together one night to have a few drinks and hang out. At some point in the evening, they convince one person to go into a darkened bathroom holding only a candle. Once there, they are to turn around, slowly, three times. On each turn they are to say the name "Bloody Mary".

When they complete the final turn, they are supposed to face the mirror and, if they did everything right, the image of Bloody Mary will appear to them. They can then ask the image a question about the future and she will answer it.

Well, as with most things in life, it doesn't work out the way it's planned and Mary appears alright, but she's not in the mood to answer any questions. Furious at having been summoned from her eternal resting place, Mary crawls out of the mirror and rips the offending party to shreds. She then returns to her place behind the mirror to await her next victim.

As with most urban legends, there are variations to the story, but you get the idea. The story of Bloody Mary seems to have found its beginnings in the 1800s.

Back in the day, young women were encouraged to take a look into the future to find their soulmate. They were told that they could achieve this if, sometime after nightfall, they would light a candle and walk backwards towards a mirror.

Once they reached the mirror, they were to turn around and shine the candle at their reflection. The face of the man they would someday marry would be illuminated in the mirror. If a skull appeared instead of a man's face, well, the girl needn't worry about marriage or a future. She would die before ever having the chance to wed.

The stories of the prophetic mirror eventually morphed into the legend of Bloody Mary as we know it today. Although, there have never been any recorded cases of a blood soaked woman being called forth from a mirror to wreak havoc on the unlucky soul who summoned her, there is a physiological basis for the story.

Apparently, if one stands in a darkened room and stares into a mirror long enough, hallucinations may result. Facial features can appear distorted or disfigured. Some people even claim that their reflections become those of animal faces instead of their own.

Our minds are fragile things and they can be easily tricked into seeing things that aren't really there, as in this case. The hallucinations are akin to a sort of self-hypnosis. Our faces don't really change, but the prolonged staring, coupled with dim lighting, rewires our brains into sending our eyes images that aren't really there.

Needless to say, don't try this at home. It can't be good for you, either physically or mentally. I'm simply relating information. I didn't test it. My own reflection is scary enough. I don't need to make it any worse.

One last thought on the subject of mirrors. People prone to superstition will tell you that mirrors are something not to be toyed with. Some folks believe that when a person dies, their soul looks for refuge in the nearest portal. That is why, in the past, mirrors would be immediately covered with sheets when someone died, thus preventing the departing soul from taking up residence there.

Could that old wives tale also have contributed to the legend of Bloody Mary? It is possible, given the belief that mirrors can harbor the spirits of those who have passed on. Maybe someone, at some point in time, caught a glimpse of one of those trapped souls while staring into a mirror for too long. That's why antique mirrors are a thing to be avoided. It's said that one can never know what that mirror has seen or what might be captured behind the glass.

Chapter 8:
The Killer in the Backseat

A woman driving along a lonely stretch of highway stops at a gas station to refuel. The attendant lingers at her car for an uncomfortable length of time. He keeps looking at the woman in a fashion that makes her uneasy.

The attendant pumps the gas and the woman hands him her credit card. The creepy attendant takes the card and walks into the station to complete the sale. He returns moments later and informs her that the card was declined. The bank is on the phone and they need to speak to her.

The woman doesn't want to leave the safety of her car and step out into the night with this odd character so she argues. She tells him that she will use a different card. He won't hear of it. The attendant insists that she come inside with him. He tells her that the card was reported stolen and he will call the police if she doesn't come with him right away.

Not knowing what else to do and not wanting any trouble, the woman reluctantly gets out of her car and follows the attendant into the service station. Once inside, he locks the door behind them. It's not the bank on the phone, it's the police.

The attendant informs the woman that when he went to pump the gas, he noticed a man crouched down in the backseat of her car. Worse still, the man was holding a hatchet. The woman had narrowly escaped death, thanks to the observant gas station attendant.

It's every woman's nightmare come true. If it is indeed a true story and not just a cautionary tale passed down from one generation to another. The stories of the killer in the backseat can be traced back to the 1960s. They began with a true story, but it barely resembles the urban legend it became.

The original story took place in New York City in 1964. It involved an escaped murderer on the lam who decided to hide in the first car he could find. After making entry, he had lain down behind the seats and waited for the driver. His plan was allegedly to commandeer the vehicle and, once he was in the clear, dispatch the luckless witness.

When his mark finally arrived, things didn't go as planned. The car's owner turned out to be an off-duty NYC police officer who shot the escaped con soon after he popped up from his hiding place in the backseat.

Stories of killers lying in wait for unsuspecting drivers can be found all over the world. While the details may vary, they all end virtually the same way. The driver—usually a woman—is saved by a knight in shining armor before she can come to any harm.

In one well-worn variation, a lone female is driving along a dark, dreary highway late at night when she notices a car speeding up behind her. When the other driver is upon her, he begins to flash his lights and honk the horn intermittently. Scared out of her wits, she accelerates, hoping to lose the madman who is tailing her.

At some point, the car pulls up beside her. When she makes eye contact with the driver, she sees that he is pointing toward the back of her car and motioning frantically for her to pull over. Fearing that something is wrong with one of her tires, she veers onto the side of the road, followed closely by the excitable stranger.

The minute she comes to a stop, the man jumps out of his car and, without saying a word, grabs her by the arm and hurries her to his vehicle. Before she has time to react, he pushes her inside and locks the door behind her.

Once she is out of harm's way, he explains that he had observed a suspicious figure in the backseat of her car. Sensing that she was unaware that her life could be in danger, he had flashed his lights and honked the horn every time he saw the man's head rise up, causing him to duck out of sight.

As the woman and her rescuer speed away, she looks back to see a man emerging from the backseat of her car. As he stands just off the road, illuminated by the headlights, she can see a knife gleaming in his hand.

The 'killer in the backseat' anecdotes probably started as warnings to motorists, especially women traveling alone, to be aware of their surroundings. Always check your car before you get in lest someone be hiding somewhere inside, and remember to keep your doors locked.

These cautionary tales serve as reminders that, contrary to how things play out in the world of urban legends, there may not always be someone there to save you from an opportunistic killer. Good advice—then and now.

Chapter 9:
Alligators in the Sewer

Mutant alligators have been rumored to roam the vast sewer systems that run beneath the streets of New York City since the 1920s. As the stories go, baby alligators are purchased at souvenir shops by families vacationing down South. Once the alligators start to mature, the people no longer want them so they flush them down the toilet. The alligators manage to survive their ordeal and eventually make a life for themselves in the drainage pipes and cesspools under the city.

The question is, is it possible that such a thing could happen? Apparently, yes it is, at least in part. It is true that, in the 1920s and 30s, you could buy a baby alligator and try to turn it into a family pet. Since alligators can grow as large as fourteen feet long and weigh in excess of five hundred pounds; most people didn't keep the pets for long.

Even so, flushing them down the toilet seems a bit of a stretch. It's more likely that they were released into drainage ditches when no one was looking. It wasn't long before sewer workers began reporting seeing alligators swimming in the sewage and lying around in the drainage pipes.

At first, these sightings were met with disbelief. The city's stand on the issue of alligators roaming the sewer system was that it was impossible. The workers were imagining things. They were told to just do their jobs and let the matter drop.

The workers knew better. They began to keep logs of sightings of alligators until there had been so many reports that the city had to take action. A team of experts decided to check the stories out for themselves and, lo and behold, when they shone their lights through the darkness they saw glowing eyes illuminated everywhere. The system was literally crawling with alligators.

Exterminators and sharp shooters were called in and the gators were systematically killed off. By 1937, the sewers beneath New York City were officially declared alligator free. Still, from time to time, sightings of alligators under the city are still reported. Since it isn't as easy to purchase an alligator today as it was almost a hundred years ago, it would be hard to explain how they got there. It is possible that not all of the original gators were killed in the mass extermination of 1937. Perhaps, some of the descendants still lay claim to the underground city sewers.

It's hard to believe that anything could survive in the muck and filth of a sanitation system, but alligators did quite well there. There were plenty of rats and garbage to feed on, there was no shortage of water, it was cool and dark and best of all, people were scarce in the underbelly of the city. Alligators can live to be fifty years old so it is conceivable that some of the offspring of the original gators still reside in their home away from home.

To this day, there are people who claim that some of the alligators mutated into monsters. There have been reports of albino specimens that have lost skin pigment from all of the years spent underground in the pitch darkness. The reptiles had also lost something else they no longer needed, namely, their eyes. All the same, no albino alligators have ever been retrieved from the sewer system.

Toxic waste is also a hazard in the bowels of the city which gave rise to another rumor. Supposedly, some of the alligators had fed on dangerous chemical-laden garbage that had turned them into something monstrous. They had mutated into something one would only see in a horror or science fiction movie. Giant, lumbering creatures with red eyes and oozing skin were supposedly seen by some of the sewer workers. Of course, no one could ever pin down exactly who the witnesses were.

Once again, this is an urban legend that grew from an actual incident. There really were alligators in the sewer system under the city of New York. The legend did begin with people disposing of baby gators they had purchased as pets. The alligators survived and thrived in the dark, damp underground. That is until they were exterminated, for the most part, in the 1930s.

It is possible that a few surviving alligators still roam the tunnels and drains beneath the city. There are areas of the system that are rarely seen by humans, so the chance does exist, however remote, that things we'd rather not think about live just below us, unseen and undisturbed, and have for nearly a century.

Chapter 10:
The Mole People

Alligators aren't the only outcasts rumored to live in the dark recesses of the "Big Apple." There is also a city beneath the city, if the stories are to be believed. This underground community is said to be inhabited by a large group of social misfits who are known as "The Mole People."

Stories of underground dwellers have circulated for decades. It began when a few vagrants began living in the subway tunnels. When that situation became too crowded, some of the people moved deeper beneath the city.

They set up tents in the darkness of the underground. They used oil lamps for light, eventually connecting into the city's electrical system so they could use lamps. More and more of the disenfranchised began setting up camp under the city. Soon, they numbered in the hundreds.

As the population grew, the need for law and order became clear. A mayor was elected to oversee the citizens. Crime was rampant so groups of enforcers were assigned to keep the peace. Some of the mole people were college graduates who had never been in trouble in their lives. They had lost their way or become disenchanted with society and decided to begin anew in what they hoped would be an underground Utopia.

Many of the other residents weren't so clean-cut. They were drug addicts, alcoholics and criminals of all varieties. People were robbed, beaten and worse. It became an impossible task to keep order in the city under the city. Utopia soon became a dangerous place and some of its citizens returned to living above ground.

Authorities were also aware of the mole people and their illegal activities. Living beneath the city is not allowed and police officers were sent in on occasion to round up the underground dwellers and send them packing. The "moles" would wait until they felt the coast was clear and then return to their dark, damp existence.

Are mole people real or just an urban legend? It is true that there are people who attempt to live underneath the city. The homeless and desperate sometimes make their way into the underground tunnels and live there for as long as they can until they are forced to move on.

Sleeping in the subway is a far cry from establishing an underground city complete with law enforcement and political parties. Have some members of society become so fed up that they decide to start a whole new civilization in the darkness that lies beneath a major metropolis? Or, has the situation of a few vagrants who found their way underneath the city been exaggerated?

Chapter 11:
The Earwig

What could be more horrifying than an encounter with the dreaded earwig? Never heard of one? Take a seat and make yourself comfortable, you are in for a treat.

In tales of lore, the earwig is a burrowing insect that hides away under the bed clothes of its unfortunate victim. While their host sleeps peacefully, the earwig crawls into their ear and begins to feed. The ravenous appetite of the night parasite is only sated when they reach the other side and exit through the opposite ear from which they entered. You see, an earwig can't turn around or walk backwards, so the only way out is to eat everything in their path, which in this case, is the victim's brain.

Few people survive a visit from an earwig. Those who do, suffer agonizing pain for days or weeks afterward as their damaged minds attempt to heal. As awful as that is, the worst is yet to come.

There is always the possibility that the earwig was a female. You see, females lay eggs—millions of them—and what better place to nest than in the soft tissues of the human brain? The female earwig deposits her eggs and then exits the oblivious host's ear. Only later will the recipient realize what has happened to him and by then it's too late.

For the unfortunate victim who survives the initial encounter with the female earwig; a fate worse than death is waiting just around the corner. Once the eggs hatch, millions of tiny offspring will pollute their brain. And, make no mistake, they are born hungry. The creatures feed ravenously on the victim's brain, the gnawing of the earwigs driving them to madness before death mercifully takes them.

This disturbing scenario is loosely based on an episode of a popular 1970s anthology series, but stories of the earwig can be found in folklore throughout the ages. Many of us, after first hearing of the earwig, slept with our ears covered lest one of the tiny killers be lurking in the darkness waiting to crawl in and feast on our brains.

The truth of the matter is that there really are such things as earwigs. They're a nasty-looking critter with wings they seldom use and pincers that resemble forceps on their abdomens. Just as in the legend, they do prefer to feed at night, but this is where the similarities end.

Earwigs are rather reclusive insects that like to find dark places to hide until the sun goes down and they can wander off in search of a meal. Their menu of choice includes other insects, flowers and, to the great annoyance of farmers, crops.

There are over two thousand species of earwigs that can be found scattered all over the globe. In Old English, the word earwig means "ear beetle." They are so named not because they like to burrow into ears, but because, when unfolded, their wings look very much like a human ear.

Earwigs do end up in strange places on occasion. The odd earwig might find its way into a sleeping person's ear purely by chance. Contrary to their reputation, they can and do turn around or back their way out. The ones that can't manage this feat on their own are usually extracted in a doctor's office with a pair of tweezers.

The earwig's pincers look menacing, but are pretty harmless to humans. They rarely pierce human skin, and if they do, it's no worse than a pin-prick. They are not particularly aggressive and pose no threat apart from their penchant for destroying the occasional crop.

We know now that earwigs are not, as some horror writers would have you believe, gluttons who feed on humans. They prefer flowers to brains with the odd insect thrown in for good measure.

All the same, if a wandering earwig happens to find its way into your ear in the dead of night, make a mad dash for the tweezers. The tightrope between fact and fiction is a tenuous one and this is the perfect example of a line better left uncrossed.

Chapter 12:
The Rat King

Rat, or rodent, kings have been around for hundreds of years. Legend has it that when too many rats are confined to a small place, their tails eventually get tangled together thus forming one large mutated rodent known as a "rat king." This can also occur with mice and squirrels, but rats are the most common subjects of this phenomenon.

The mass collection of conjoined rats is called a rat king because, supposedly, the leader of the rat colony will then rest upon the tangle of tails and rule over the rat population. In actuality, it isn't the rats that are connected to one another that claim the title of king, but rather the wise rodent who sits on the throne made up of his gnarled pile of followers.

Stories of rat kings are not common in the United States, but they are popular throughout Europe. No live rat kings have ever been captured, but curiosity seekers have found dead ones. There are even rat king specimens, some mummified, on display in natural museums in Germany and France.

To see a living rat king is considered bad luck. Terrible things are said to befall anyone who crosses paths with the conjoined pack of rats who serve their king. They are a bad omen. It has been recorded that rat kings were sighted just before outbreaks of plague and other devastating diseases.

Could rat kings really occur naturally? It's unlikely given that rats are remarkably intelligent creatures. If they did, indeed, live in such overcrowded surroundings that their tails got tangled together, they would surely chew through them in order to escape.

The idea that a group of rats would sit by and do nothing as their tails interlocked is a bit far-fetched. It's more likely that rat king specimens that have been found and put on display are products of human intervention. Since the rat king only seems to turn up once all of the members have perished, it would be surprising to find a live tangle of rats surviving in such a situation, but not impossible. Rats, as we all know, are extremely adaptable creatures.

Chapter 13:
The Boogeyman

No exploration into the world of urban legends would be complete without a look at the one that started them all: the boogeyman. He exists everywhere and nowhere. He's under the bed, hiding in the closet, or waiting just outside the window for parents to leave the room so he can feast on their fat, juicy children.

The boogeyman legend is as old as time. In every corner of the globe and in nearly every culture, there is some version of the boogeyman. He is eternal. He is that thing in the darkness that we dare not speak of. He is your worst nightmare come to life.

It is nearly impossible to say for sure when and where the boogeyman originated. He was surely conjured up as a tool to get children to mind their parents or else the boogeyman would get them. Many a parent has used this legend when all else fails. They will caution their children: "Don't stay out past your curfew or the boogeyman will be waiting for you." Or utilize the old standby: "Do as I say or I'll sic the boogeyman on you."

So, who is the boogeyman? He is whatever scares you the most. If you're frightened of demons, that's who he is for you. If bears terrify you, he will come to you in the form of a bear. The worst thing your mind can conjure up is exactly how he will appear to you.

Sometimes, the boogeyman is just a dark shape passing through a room. At other times, he is eyes that stare out from a crack in the closet door. Every kid knows that the boogeyman can be anywhere. That is why you have to keep the covers pulled up around your neck and—whatever you do—don't let your legs dangle off of the side of the bed. That's just asking for the boogeyman to drag you off to someplace far away where no one will hear your screams.

As scary as all of the boogeyman stories are, they are just fantasy, at least up to a point. There have certainly been many cases over the years of real-life boogeymen that have done things more terrifying than any make believe monster ever could.

One of those monsters was a man named Tommy Lynn Sells who was executed by the state of Texas in 2014 for the brutal murder of thirteen-year-old Kaylene Harris. He was every parent's worst nightmare: a devil in human form who preyed upon the most innocent of victims.

Sells was thought to have been responsible for the murders of at least twenty-two men, women and children. It wasn't until the attack on young Kaylene and her friend Krystal Surles that his reign of terror finally came to an end.

The killer had been an acquaintance of Kaylene's parents. When they met him at a community church event, he was down on his luck and, being good people, they tried to help him in any way they could. They couldn't know that their kindness would be repaid with more heartache than they imagined possible.

It was on New Year's Eve, 1999, that the family saw what the real Tommy Lynn Sells was capable of. As Kaylene and Krystal were sleeping peacefully in Kaylene's bunk beds, Sells crept into the room and began to viciously attack the thirteen-year-old.

Awakened by the violence taking place in the bed below hers, ten-year-old Krystal watched helplessly as her friend was stabbed multiple times. When Sells was finished with Kaylene, he turned his attention to Krystal; slicing the child across the throat.

Thinking that both girls were dead, he fled the scene. Young Krystal, though critically wounded, managed to escape from the home and make it to a neighbor's house. They immediately called police and the search for the maniac who attacked the girls was set into motion.

Kaylene did not survive the horrifying attack, but Krystal did, and she remembered everything. With her help, a forensic artist was able to draw a sketch of what the killer looked like. Before long, authorities had their man: one Tommy Lynn Sells.

Sells admitted to killing Kaylene and attempting to murder Krystal. He didn't stop there. He confessed to murders all over the country, as well as other unspeakable crimes. He was the devil incarnate for anyone unfortunate enough to encounter him when he was on a crime spree.

Still recovering from the injuries that had nearly killed her, Krystal testified against Sells at his murder trial. He was convicted of the murder of Kaylene as well as the attempted murder of Krystal. He received the ultimate punishment: death by lethal injection. Krystal's nightmare was finally over. This boogeyman would never hurt her or anyone else ever again.

There are also boogeymen that are the products of the worldwide communication highway we call the internet. The most famous, or infamous, of those has to be Slender Man.

Slender Man began innocently enough as an internet meme. Not long after his creation, various web sites started inviting users to send in their own Slender Man stories. People from all over the world began to make up scary tales with this new threat at their center.

In many of the fictionalized accounts, Slender Man was a nameless, faceless entity who stalked and sometimes murdered unsuspecting victims. He was usually portrayed as very tall and thin with abnormally long limbs.

Video games and even film shorts have been developed with Slender Man as their central character. He has become a phenomenon very popular with teens and adults alike. As with anything that becomes as well-known as Slender Man, some people took it too seriously, with dire consequences.

In May of 2014, two twelve-year-old girls in Wisconsin invited a mutual friend over for a sleepover. The friend had spent time at the home of one of the girls before and they were good friends. She had no reason to think that this night would be any different. She couldn't have been more wrong.

The two girls who had suggested the sleepover had a plan. They were going to isolate the third girl and then, when the time was right, kill her. They weren't angry with the girl. In fact, they had no problems with her whatsoever. Allegedly, they wanted to kill their friend to prove to Slender Man that they were worthy to be his disciples.

The girls had followed the exploits of Slender Man online and believed him to be real. They thought that he lived in the woods somewhere close by. They intended to murder their friend and then find his house so they could reveal to him what they had done.

Once the two girls had the third girl alone, one of them is said to have held her down while the other one stabbed her.

Thinking that they had accomplished their mission, they left the girl's body in the woods and set out looking for Slender Man.

A passing bicyclist happened upon the girl who had been so brutally attacked by those she thought were her friends. The girl had been stabbed over a dozen times, but she was still alive and was even able to identify her assailants.

The pair of would-be killers were quickly apprehended and are still awaiting trial. Their alleged victim is still recovering both physically and emotionally from what happened to her that day when her friends turned on her for a boogeyman that existed only in their minds.

The boogeyman of the past is a creature from the land of make believe whose original purpose was to get kids to walk the straight and narrow and mind their elders. That doesn't mean that there aren't plenty of things that go bump in the night to be fearful of, like the cold-blooded killer who unleashed his rage on two young girls one dark Texas night.

Human monsters, unlike their fictionalized counterparts, are all around us. Usually, we don't even realize how close we've come to danger until it has already passed us by. So, the next time you shiver for no apparent reason, or gooseflesh suddenly rises on your arms, keep in mind that something might be trying to tell you that evil is closer than you think.

Chapter 14:
The Stolen Kidney

A man, or woman, meets an attractive stranger in a bar. They go to a hotel and spend the night together. The next morning, he or she wakes up either on a blood-soaked bed or in the bath tub. They are in terrible pain and notice a long, ugly incision along the side of their body. They find their way to a hospital only to learn that they are missing a kidney.

That frightening urban legend began circulating in the 1990s. There are no documented cases of that particular scenario on record, but organ theft is very real. It happens, and the circumstances aren't too far removed from what you've just read.

In 2008, an organ theft ring was discovered in India. One victim, Mohammed Salim Khan, arrived at a hospital just outside of Delhi with quite a story to tell. Khan, a day laborer, claimed that he had been approached on the street by a man offering him construction work. Never one to turn down a job, Khan jumped at the chance. He had five children to support and the money would put food in their mouths.

Khan was taken to a house by his new employer, but once there, instead of finding work, he was given an injection that knocked him out. For several days, he was held at gunpoint and subjected to various blood tests and screenings. Still, he was being fed and had a roof over his head, so he went along in the hopes that the construction job would still materialize.

The next thing he remembers is waking up with a terrible pain in his belly. A man in surgical garb was standing over him. When Khan asked what was happening, the 'doctor' informed him that they had removed one of his kidneys.

A thoroughly shaken Khan was warned that if he told anyone about the kidney theft or anything else that had occurred at the house, he would be killed. He was informed that people would be watching him at all times and they would know if he went to the authorities.

After being released from the house, he made his way to the hospital. An MRI showed that he was indeed missing a kidney. Word of the organ theft began to spread around the city and more men started coming forward claiming the same thing had happened to them.

Stories began to come out that several men, mostly day laborers, had been offered work only to be taken to a house with a fully functional operating room. There, they would undergo several medical screenings before being taken to surgery. Afterwards, they would be told that they now had only one kidney.

The house was raided and, sure enough, police found an operating room just as the men had described. Kidneys were being harvested and then sold on the black market. The organs stolen from the day laborers were being sold all over the world. The masterminds were getting rich while the men who had lost their kidneys were so debilitated by the surgeries that most were unable to work. They could no longer support their families because of this nightmare they had unwittingly stepped into.

The organ theft ring was shut down, but that was little comfort to Khan and others like him. Worse yet, it is thought that similar rings still operate all over the world. This is just one kidney theft horror story, there are many more that have come to light and still more that go unpunished.

So, even though the urban legend of the smitten bar patron who wakes up without a kidney is a stretch, organ theft is very real. It has happened in the past and is probably still happening today. There is no shortage of depraved individuals who will take advantage of the poor and desperate if given the chance. Money is money to them, even if it is covered in an innocent man's blood.

Chapter 15:
The Cursed Painting

At one time or another in your life, you've probably read a scary story or watched a horror movie in which a statue or painting came to life. Such a thing, as we all know, is not possible. That is, of course, if we keep our minds firmly planted in the realm of logic. The following events occurred someplace outside of that safety net; a place where all that we know of the world is set aside and something truly remarkable, and terrifying, takes over.

This story first came to light in February of 2000 when a piece of art, known in the world of urban legends as "The Haunted Painting," went up for sale on a popular online auction site. Titled *The Hands Resist Him*, the work depicts a young boy standing in front of what appears to be a storefront or tenement building. The doors behind him boast a number of glass panes. On the other side of the glass, eleven hands can be seen pressed up against the windows.

The boy is not alone in the painting. Standing off to his right, is a life-size doll. His companion sports a blue dress, wavy brown hair and blank eyes that stare ahead at nothing and everything. In her hands, she holds a discombobulated cell battery; its wires springing madly in all directions.

The sellers of the unique art piece posted a disclaimer along with the listing. According to them, the painting was cursed. They implored buyers to look the other way if they were fearful of the supernatural. This item, they assured the public, was not for everyone.

If their claims were to be believed, the two figures that were featured in the painting had the ability to leave the canvas whenever the notion struck them. The boy especially could not be contained. The owners believed that he often stepped out of the imaginary world and into the real one in order to escape the thing he feared most, namely, the doll.

To back up their claim, the sellers included stills that appeared to show the exact same painting with one glaring omission. The disembodied hands were still present, as was the doll, but the boy had vanished from the scene.

Apparently, that hadn't been the only time that the painting had transformed. The listers alleged that they had witnessed a scenario in which the doll could be seen holding an object in her hand other than the battery. According to them, she had been pointing what appeared to be a gun at the terrified boy as he tried desperately to find a way off of the canvas.

Normally, such an unlikely scenario would have been dismissed as a hoax or ploy to ensure snaring the highest bidder. In this case, as unbelievable as it seemed, people sat up and took notice. One reason was the visceral reaction that many experienced when they viewed the image online.

Over thirty-thousand potential buyers saw the listing and, in turn, the pictures of the item itself. An alarming number of people who laid eyes on the depiction of the boy and the doll suffered attacks of nausea, dizziness, vivid dreams, night terrors and severe anxiety soon afterwards.

One young woman who viewed the original listing with her father claimed that, just as she declared the story to be a ridiculous hoax, all of the lights in the house suddenly went out. All that is, except for the one that continued to illuminate the computer screen as it displayed the image of the boy and his doll.

Even with its questionable history, the painting sold for $1,025. The lucky buyer was Perception Gallery in Grand Rapids, Michigan. Curious about the painting's beginnings, the curator contacted the artist who had been responsible for the infamous work.

Bill Stoneham was surprised when he received the first of many communications from the gallery owner. When informed of the painting's supposed dark history, Stoneham had no explanation as to why the piece he had created in 1972 had been a source of distress for its owners.

The artist did offer one bit of trivia that caught the curator off-guard. Stoneham mentioned, matter-of-factly, that the owner of the first gallery to have featured the painting died prematurely, as did the art critic who attended the first public showing.

When asked to explain any deep meaning behind *The Hands Resist Him,* Stoneham said that he had been inspired to create the piece after coming across a childhood photo of himself taken at the age of five.

The hands that can be seen reaching from behind the glass represented opportunities, both taken and missed. Every road available in life was meant to be presented by those hands that reached out from nowhere and implored the boy to decide which paths to take. The child, with his back turned to the myriad of possibilities, is unaware of what is being offered.

The doll's purpose was to act as a guide for the boy. She was sent to lead him along life's pathways. If those who owned the painting in later years were correct, she abandoned that role for another. In the end, she acted as his captor, keeping the boy bound to one place for eternity.

It is theorized that this is why the battery has been destroyed, the wires all pulled out. What had been intended as a power source for the doll was no longer needed once she began to draw strength from a sinister force, as yet unknown.

Born in Boston, Stoneham had been given up for adoption at birth. He spent nearly a year in an orphanage before finding loving parents to call his own. Soon, the newly formed family settled into a quiet life in the Midwest.

Stoneham spent his early years in Chicago where, by all accounts, he led a completely normal and relatively uneventful life. No dark secrets or ominous occurrences tainted his upbringing. Nothing in his past would lead one to believe that he possessed the power to breathe life into images with the stroke of a brush.

It had been Stoneham's first wife who had coined the phrase that would inspire the title of the infamous work. She wrote a poem that lamented her husband's time spent at the orphanage being passed over again and again as he waited to be chosen. She had named her prose, *The Hands Resist Him.*

In order to support his family, Stoneham had taken work as a commissioned artist in the early 1970s. It was during this period that he painted what would become his magnum opus. Upon its completion, *The Hands Resist Him* was displayed at the Feingarten Art Gallery in Beverly Hills, California.

Los Angeles Times art critic Henry Seldis was the first to view and critique the painting. He would die by his own hand in

1978 at the age of fifty-two. Charles Feingarten, the gallery owner, passed away three years later at age sixty from unknown causes.

The next owner of the painting was actor John Marley. He is probably best known for his roles in *The Godfather* and as Ali McGraw's father in *Love Story*. In the former, he was the unlucky fellow who woke up to find that he was sharing his bed with the decapitated head of a horse.

Marley kept the painting for several years before selling it. He died from complications following open heart surgery not long after passing on ownership of the artwork.

The couple who would eventually list the piece on the auction site, originally purchased it to adorn the walls of their daughter's bedroom. Since it depicted a child and a doll, the painting had, for them, looked like something that a four-year old would enjoy seeing in her small world. They would soon learn that this would not be the case.

From the very beginning, the youngster showed an aversion to the painting. She claimed that she couldn't sleep because the boy and doll fought all night long. She also asserted that the boy would crawl out of the painting to escape the wrath of the doll.

The child's parents were aware that four-year-olds are prone to flights of fancy and imagination. Even so, her reactions had been so extreme that they decided to set up motion-detecting cameras in their daughter's room. If the boy was indeed exiting the painting, they wanted to capture the events on film.

Sure enough, three nights after the camera was put in use, footage was obtained of the boy hopping down off of the canvas and scrambling around the room, looking for a means of escape. Unable to find an out, he eventually returned to his rightful place beside the doll. For her part, the doll seemed to be able to move about in the painting, but could not leave the perimeter of the frame.

It all sounds impossible, but the film is said to exist. Whether those who claim to have seen it are being truthful or not is unclear. One thing is indisputable, once the family viewed the footage they chose to remove the painting from their home forever.

The gallery that now owns the artwork keeps it locked away for the good of everyone. They have been offered staggering amounts of money for the piece, but have refused all bids. As of this writing, it remains secured someplace where it can do no harm.

Those who have seen the painting first-hand claim that babies cry uncontrollably in its presence. Children shy away from the images. Adults have said that they lose time while in the company of the piece. When they regain their senses, they have no recollection of how much time has passed or what occurred in the interim. Some observers have sworn that they felt they were being touched by invisible hands, presumably those depicted in the painting.

Whether or not *The Hands Resist Him* is indeed a cursed object that somehow brings painted figures to life or simply an elaborate hoax perpetrated by a series of owners is up for debate. What is known is that the work has caused a wide-range of physical and mental reactions in people from all over the world.

Some believe that the painting and the powers it allegedly possesses are the result of mass hysteria. After all, when one is told over and over again that an object has qualities that cannot be explained, it is natural to look for those very things. If you expect a painting to make you feel ill, perhaps it will because you, unwittingly, make it so.

There is always the chance, of course, that the painting is everything it is said to be. Art is an amazing and mysterious force. Who's to say that the hand of the artist doesn't pass a piece of his or her soul into a work with each swipe of the brush?

Perhaps in the dark reaches of his being, in a place he didn't even know existed, Bill Stoneham summoned entities that now reside inside his masterpiece. Trapped between worlds, the boy and doll are forever bound together, at least as long as the painting remains intact.

Chapter 16:
The Red Spot

When the general public is asked to name their greatest fear, spiders always rank near the top. Although most of these ominous looking little buggers are harmless to humans, something about them strikes terror in the hearts of even the bravest souls. Given their reputation, it's natural that a story involving spiders would figure prominently in the world of urban legends. If creepy crawlers of any kind make you squeamish, you might want to skip to the next chapter.

This unsettling tale began circulating around Europe in the 1970s. The horrifying ordeal was said to have started when a vacationer, usually a woman, is bitten by a spider while sunbathing on a beach.

The traveler feels the stabbing sensation on her cheek, but doesn't give the incident too much thought. She pulls out a compact from her bag and examines the area. The woman is relieved to see that the damage is minimal. The only evidence of the bite is a tiny red dot the size of a pinprick.

Later that evening while lounging in her hotel room, the vacationer suddenly feels a sharp pain in the effected cheek. She runs to the bathroom and switches on the light above the mirror. To her horror, she sees that the spot has grown several times in size in only a couple of hours.

As the time ticks by, the wound continues to grow. As if that wasn't bad enough, the woman begins to get the feeling that something is moving around just under the skin. When she again takes a look at the site in the mirror, she is sent into a panic by what she observes.

What started off as a miniscule dot had transformed into a festering wound that was now larger than a golf ball. Worse still, any attempt she makes to apply ointment to the area is met with a pain so severe that it brings her to her knees.

The woman's swollen cheek torments her well into the night. At some point, she realizes that she needs to seek medical attention. As she gets dressed and prepares to leave her hotel room, she feels the entire side of her face heat up as if it is on fire.

Rushing to the bathroom once again, she gazes at her now unrecognizable reflection in the mirror. As she watches in disbelief, her cheek bursts open and thousands of tiny spiders flow out of the wound.

The woman is so traumatized by the event that she has to be committed to a psychiatric institution. Her fear of spiders, from that point on, makes living in society impossible. As far as anyone knows, she remains confined to a hermetically sealed room where no insects, or arachnids, can enter.

Another version of this legend involves a woman who is bitten on the cheek as she sleeps. She awakens to find a red spot on her face, but is not aware of the culprit who left the mark. As the day progresses, the bite turns angry.

The woman doesn't take action until later on in the afternoon when the area begins to swell. As the wound grows in size, she can't help but acknowledge that something is moving inside of her bulbous cheek.

Knowing that steam can cause a boil to rupture, the victim runs a scalding hot bath and submerges herself in the water. As the intense heat envelops her face, activity within the swollen area reaches a breaking point, literally.

As the woman lies soaking in the tub, the agonizing lesion suddenly ruptures sending a horde of hatchling spiders spilling into the bath water. The sight is so horrifying that the young woman never fully recovers from the experience.

In reality, there are no recorded cases of spiders laying their eggs inside of humans. That is not to say, however, that other creepy-crawly things don't use us as incubators for their broods.

There are a surprising number of insects that are capable of crawling inside of an unwilling host. The African loa loa, or eye worm, enters the body by way of the bite from a deer fly. Once inside the warm, wet environment, the female releases embryos by the thousands.

As they develop, these tiny beings travel through the body, a process that can take years, until they find an exit. During this time, they can often be seen moving along under the skin of the host. As if that weren't bad enough, at some stages of their development, they have been observed passing across the surface of the victim's eye.

As ghastly as that thought might be, it isn't the worst story of parasitic freeloaders. Several years ago, I knew a gentleman who had been bitten by a brown recluse spider while staying in a hotel room in Ohio.

The man sought treatment immediately for the painful wound that was eating away at his knee. No amount of care would heal the area which developed, over time, into a gaping hole. He kept the knee covered most of the time, but was not shy about showing the extent of his decay. He would also say, without a bit of self-pity, that he had actually observed the flesh falling away as the infection worsened.

Even though they didn't do him any good, the man remained on a course of antibiotics for several months. He also applied ointments that proved to be useless. Still, he didn't let his bad knee interfere with the things he enjoyed doing. One of his favorite pastimes was sitting on his front porch watching the comings and goings in the neighborhood.

Unfortunately, he spent hot summer days lounging on his outdoor rocking chair for hours on end. He didn't realize that during one of those lazy days, a fly had laid eggs inside of the open wound. The first time that he was aware of this was when maggots hatched in what was left of his knee.

There was a silver lining to this series of appalling events. After the incident, the man's daughter took him to a specialist in Columbus where he finally received the proper treatment. A series of skin grafts eventually gave him back something close to a proper leg. Life as he had once known it had been restored.

Much like the loa loa, botflies enter the body of a host by way of the bite of another insect, usually a mosquito. The worm gestates underneath the skin resulting in a pus-filled sore. This nasty soup nourishes the worm until it develops enough to burst into the world. This process can take up to three months to complete. In the meantime, it causes redness, itching and pain while it feeds on its living host.

Botflies are normally found in South and Central America, but its North American cousin, the warble fly, operates in much the same way. Although botflies prefer human receptacles, warble flies tend to stick to our fur-covered counterparts.

In 2013, UK resident Rochelle Harris returned home after spending some leisure time in Peru. Not long after getting settled in, she began being plagued by headaches that were accompanied by fluid draining from her ear.

Rochelle also complained that she was hearing strange noises that seemed to originate inside of her head. No one but her could hear the sounds that were beginning to drive her mad. When the never ending droning became too much for her, she decided to seek medical care.

Upon examining Rochelle, physicians made a gruesome discovery. They informed the stunned patient that a storm of maggots had hatched inside of her head. The gnawing sound that only she could hear had been the tiny parasites eating away at the interior of her ear.

It was determined that at some point during her vacation, a fly had flown into her ear and laid its eggs before departing. After some reflection, Rochelle recalled an incident in which she had walked through a cloud of flies. Presumably, this is when one of them decided to use her as a vehicle to nurture its squirming offspring.

In the end, a spider bite that results in hundreds of tiny creatures bursting forth from a person's face is extremely unlikely. On the other hand, the human body is the perfect host for other opportunistic creatures looking for a warm place in which to gestate their young.

The moral of this story is: if you ever get the feeling that something is moving around under your skin or buzzing inside of your head, put down whatever it is you're doing and get to the nearest health care facility to have it checked out. It's probably nothing, but on the off chance that you have been chosen to play surrogate to a brood of wriggling parasites, it's better to err on the side of caution.

Chapter 17:
The Dog Boy

Stories began circulating in the 1990s of a mysterious being that appeared to be a man, but walked on all fours like a dog. According to lore, this hybrid creature had once been a man who had spent his mortal life sacrificing canines to the devil in order to gain their power. As a reward for his diligent brutality, he was eventually transformed into what would be known in the annals of urban legends as "The Dog Boy."

This staple of Arkansas folklore was said to have terrorized all whom he encountered. Even after his transformation, the thing that used to be human could only be sustained by feasting on the blood of animals; his preferred victims being dogs.

People out walking their four-legged companions would report being followed by something that stayed in the shadows, just outside of their line of vision. All that they could see during the encounters was a pair of glowing eyes reflected in the moonlight.

Even though the stalker could not be seen by the person walking their dog, the pet was instantly aware that something was wrong. Normally docile animals would react violently to the thing that lurked in the darkness. The most obedient of dogs would attempt to escape its tether in a bid to either flee the scene or confront the threatening presence.

Pet owners who let their animals out to roam freely sometimes never saw them again. Some dogs that disappeared were later found mutilated or half-eaten. Before long, sightings of a large predator, thought to be to blame for the rash of killings, began to make the rounds in the community.

Those who saw the creature firsthand claimed that it appeared to be a very large man who walked on all fours. He wore tattered clothing that looked like it had not been changed in years. His face was still human, but had taken on the characteristics of a canine, most notably, a long snout.

With the passage of time, the reports died down as did the dog slayings. It was assumed that either the suspect had moved on or met its demise when it encountered prey more formidable than itself. It was also possible that the man/dog had never existed at all. That would have been the most likely scenario had it not been for the abominable acts of one of Arkansas' native sons.

Gerald Bettis was born in Quitman, Arkansas in 1954. His parents, Floyd and Alline had tried unsuccessfully for years to have a child. They had all but given up on the idea of being parents when, out of the blue, Alline found out that she was expecting.

The Bettises were approaching middle age when their tiny miracle was born. The child they never thought they'd have quickly became the center of their universe. The couple doted on Gerald to such an extent that he grew up believing that the world did, for all intents and purposes, revolve around him.

From early on, Gerald showed a penchant for cruelty that should have sent his parents scrambling for help. Instead, they chose to ignore their son's actions even when he turned his aggression on them.

Little Gerald's favorite pastime as a child was capturing and torturing animals. Concerned neighbors complained to his parents that they could hear the cries of these unfortunate souls as they were being subjected to the boy's twisted experiments.

As was their habit, Floyd and Alline made excuses for their son's behavior. The one thing they didn't do was confront Gerald. It would only upset him which was something they had learned to avoid at all cost.

The Bettises were, at least until Gerald entered the picture, considered by their neighbors to be good, Christian people. The couple had always been kind and thoughtful. What they had done to deserve the tiny terror that was Gerald was beyond anyone's comprehension.

According to locals, the boy collected so many animals that his family had to build on to their house in order to accommodate their son's hobby. Townspeople had learned over the years that they had to keep a close eye on their valued pets. To let a dog or cat out of one's sight for even a moment could leave it vulnerable to the ever watchful eye of Gerald Bettis.

Although he was merciless to any creature he deemed weaker than himself, Gerald was a perpetual victim in the human world. Relentlessly bullied at school, he cowered when in the company of his peers. Oddballs don't normally fare well on playgrounds and Gerald most assuredly fell into that category.

By the time Gerald reached adulthood, he stood well over six feet tall and weighed three hundred pounds. His parents took to spending all of their time upstairs in their room while their son had free rein of the rest of the house. The now elderly couple relied on their son to bring them food, which he did if he was feeling charitable.

It was rumored that Gerald was physically abusing his parents, but no one knew for sure since visitors were not permitted in the home by order of the suspect himself. It wasn't until their brutal family life spilled out for all to see that the suspicions were confirmed.

It is uncertain how the incident that brought the family's living situation to light began. What is known is that, at some point, Gerald had thrown his aged father out of a second story window. Floyd had clung to the ledge as panicked neighbors phoned police.

Local residents stood by helplessly while they waited for emergency personnel to arrive. From inside the house, Gerald could have easily pulled his father to safety, but he didn't offer any assistance. After all, it was he who had caused the predicament in the first place.

Floyd was rescued and, as was to be expected, made excuses for his son's violent outburst. Gerald remained in the house with no charges filed against him. The incident had—if nothing else—alerted the public that the elderly couple needed someone other than their son looking out for them.

Floyd died in 1981 under questionable circumstances. Official reports state that he passed from natural causes. Those close to the situation claim that he died at the hands of his only child. The truth, unfortunately, will probably never be known.

With only his mother left to keep him company, Gerald began spending time outside of the house. He was said to have struck fear in the hearts of locals who had the misfortune of crossing his path. They all sighted one thing in particular as being at the root of their gut reactions: his cold, dead eyes.

Gerald was described as having eyes completely devoid of emotion. They were simply dark pools that held not an ounce of humanity. If eyes are the windows to the soul, then Gerald Bettis had none. His was a body without substance.

Shortly after Floyd died, Alline suffered a fall which resulted in a broken hip. At least that was the story that Gerald told. When he visited her in the hospital, witnesses claimed that they saw him slap her as he warned the frail woman to keep her mouth shut about "what he had done."

As a result of this public display of aggression, Adult Protective Services stepped in and removed Alline from her son's care. Finally, after years of living in fear, Gerald's mother escaped the one person she had once worshipped above all others.

Gerald was arrested and tried for the assault on his mother. Under oath, Alline recounted the years of abuse both she and her husband had suffered at the hands of the son she had longed for her whole life.

Gerald Bettis was sent to prison where he died in 1988 of a drug overdose. His mother would outlive him, passing away in 1995 of natural causes. As their story ended, another was about to begin.

The family home was put up for sale as the last of the Bettis family left this earth. Subsequent owners soon reported a spate of strange phenomena that plagued the dwelling. Among the odd occurrences were lights that would be turned off at night only to be found blazing brightly come morning.

Tony Weaver and his wife purchased the property following the deaths of the former owners. He claimed that on one occasion pennies could be seen floating down the stairwell. The coins stopped and hovered in mid-air for a few seconds before all at once falling to the floor as if being dropped by unseen hands.

Weaver also reported that he had witnessed a man standing in the foyer peering into the living room. The intruder was dressed in a soldier's uniform that appeared to have been from WWI. When Tony attempted to confront the stranger, the man disappeared into thin air.

The Weavers eventually moved out of the house, although they retained ownership. Rather than living in the place fraught with bizarre activity, they opted to turn it into a rental property.

In 2003, Quinton White and his wife Stephanie moved into the house. One day, they heard a loud crash coming from upstairs. When Quinton went to investigate, he found that a stack of boards that had been piled in a corner were all standing upright in the middle of the floor.

Tony Weaver has attempted several times to sell the old Bettis house. One after another, prospective buyers are scared off before an offer can be made. Try as he might, Weaver can't seem to quiet the restless spirits long enough to ensure a sale.

On one occasion that the house was being shown, an empty reclining chair suddenly flipped back on its own as if someone had taken a seat and prepared to enjoy the upcoming show. Needless to say, the would-be buyers beat a hasty retreat.

One couple who brought their dog along for a viewing had their plans stymied when their normally adventurous pet refused to set foot passed the threshold. Others who came to see the house accompanied by their canines were met with similar outcomes. Dogs, as it happened, would have no part of the Bettis house.

While a remodeling project was in full swing, one of the contractors claimed that he had encountered a large cat with long brown hair and piercing eyes. He also noted that the animal had sported the arms and hands of a human.

In 2005, paranormal investigators descended upon the house in an attempt to find out who, or what, was at the heart of the alleged haunting. Their efforts uncovered multiple cold spots and pockets of energy in various areas of the home that indicated that a non-human entity was present.

While exploring the exterior of the home, the team reported seeing someone watching them from an upstairs window. Who the observer was remains a mystery since no one was inside the house at the time.

During the course of the investigation, contact was made with a spirit that claimed to be Gerald. Seething with hostility at the presence of the perceived interlopers, he had demanded that they get out of his house. Having said his peace, Gerald retreated and refused to communicate further.

It has been theorized that the man/dog that terrorized the area was actually Gerald Bettis in the form he assumed after death. Since he wasn't one to confide in others, no one knows for certain if the years of animal sacrifices were conducted to satisfy his sick urges or, perhaps, as offerings to a dark force in exchange for immortality.

The connection between the two entities that sullied the area, one being Gerald, the other being the human/canine hybrid, can be found in the descriptions of their eyes. Both were said to possess the unfeeling orbs of something lacking empathy of any kind. The same word was used in both cases; "soulless."

It is worth mentioning that speculation abounds that the house was cursed long before the Bettises moved in. No one knows why or how the structure gained this reputation. At any rate, some believe that the house had gifted a baby to the barren couple who had lost all hope of conceiving.

Perhaps whatever evil had attached itself to the property, found its outlet in Gerald. Unfortunately for the Bettises, the beast they brought into the world would be the source of great suffering for countless living beings, themselves included.

Whether the infamous Dog Boy was an accident of nature or a creature whose conception was instigated by forces that waited for an innocent couple who would not see the truth until it was too late, will never be known. What is certain is that Gerald Bettis, evil by chance or design, left his mark on the state of Arkansas and in the world of urban legends.

Chapter 18:
Watch at Your Own Risk

Today, anyone with a handheld camera can, more or less, transform themselves into a filmmaker. Back in the day, things weren't quite as easy for fledgling artists with no money or studio to fall back on. Still, they managed to produce independent movies, some of which resulted in surprisingly entertaining fare. One such underground gem would take on a life of its own, not only as an urban legend, but also as a piece of cinema that is as sought after as it is feared.

In 1987, writer/director Chester Novell Turner set his sights on making a movie that would shake viewers to their very core. With no official production company to back him, Turner took it upon himself to bring his vision to life.

During a time when "Blaxploitation" films were all the rage, Turner saw that the horror genre was being ignored. Putting pen to paper, he developed an anthology that would cement his place in the world of underground filmmaking. His fame would not stem from his talent as a director or the quality of his script. Rather, Turner would gain a reputation as the father of a cursed work that would haunt patrons for three decades to come.

The movie, titled *Tales from the QuadeaD Zone*, consists of three short stories. It begins with a short introduction in which a woman is seen reading aloud from a book. Her captive audience is the ghost of her dead son. The stories she is sharing are those that make up the content of the movie.

The first features a family of hillbillies who must fight to the death for food come mealtime. Those who have seen the footage say that the scene escalates into a gruesome, gore-filled free-for-all as the family tear each other apart, all for want of the last sandwich.

The second story involves the relationship between two brothers. The eldest has recently passed away leaving the younger one in what, at first, appears to be a state of debilitating grief. So overcome by sorrow is he that he sneaks into the graveyard one night and steals his brother's body.

After bringing the corpse back to the home they once shared, the younger brother dresses the rotting remains in a clown costume. Following this strange turn of events, the man spends hours berating the dead body for a laundry list of perceived wrongs that have been festering inside the younger brother since the two were children.

Once he has said all he needs to say, the younger brother carries the body outside and buries it underneath the house. As is to be expected in a horror movie, the story doesn't end there. Later that night, the reanimated corpse rises from its grave to exact its bloody revenge upon the still living—though not for long—younger sibling.

The third in the series is a wraparound tale that brings the film to a close. Once again, the woman who is entertaining her son with these anything but soothing tales is seen being confronted by her angry spouse.

The man is livid, apparently due to the fact that she is reading gory stories to someone who is no longer living. He becomes abusive, so much so that it compels her to match his rage with her own. The woman subsequently kills the husband before turning her weapon of choice, a knife, on herself. The film ends with the narrator slitting her own throat.

Upon its completion, the director decided to screen his cinematic endeavor to small groups in order to judge how successful he had been at putting his ideas on film. Things didn't go as he had planned. Moviegoers were certainly affected by what they saw, but not in the way Turner had intended.

Rumors circulated early on that test audiences who had been invited to screenings complained of feeling dizzy and nauseous after seeing the film. The affected parties stressed that their reactions were not due to the stories or quality of the work. No one could pinpoint the reason, but something about the movie was making otherwise healthy people sick within the span of an hour.

After he was allegedly threatened with lawsuits by some of the sufferers, Turner took it upon himself to re-edit the film. After watering down much of the violence, he felt that it was now safe to make the tape available to the public.

Only one hundred copies of the film were produced and marketed. Citing a lack of funds, the VHS release was limited to the Chicago area. By the time it hit the streets, Turner's effort had already garnered a reputation as being something more than simply an independent movie. Word of mouth touted this horror film as managing to do what no other had: harness evil and release it into the minds of those who watched it.

As it turned out, Turner's attempt to alleviate the issues associated with his work had failed. Much like the test audiences, people who purchased and viewed the tape were taken ill shortly afterwards. Somehow, a low-budget movie shot on a camcorder had gotten under their skin in ways no one could have predicted.

Since only a relatively small number of tapes had been purchased, the brouhaha died down over time. Many of those who owned a copy destroyed the offending object which seemed to alleviate their symptoms. Those who held onto the videotapes normally watched them only once. What happened to them afterwards is something only they would know.

In 2005, the story was revived when Turner's niece decided to have a yard sale. One of the items that she sold that day was an old VHS tape that she had no use for. She was not aware that the innocent blunder would reignite an urban legend that had been mostly forgotten.

The tape is considered a treasure among believers in the power it holds. It is said that the copy purchased at the sale has been making the rounds in underground film circles ever since. As the story goes, those who view the tape are often driven to the brink of insanity by what they witness.

Those who choose to watch the movie in its entirety, do so only after being given one last chance to back out. A warning posted before the opening credits supposedly cautions viewers against watching the scenes that are about to unfold

At a running time of just over an hour, *Tales from the QuadeaD Zone* is a short piece that, if the legend is true, has effects that last long after the closing credits have rolled. Even so, copies of the rare piece of guerilla filmmaking are said to be worth thousands of dollars to collectors.

Turner has, to date, only produced two films, only the first of which is said to be cursed. Why or how what began as an innocent film project snowballed into an urban legend is anyone's guess. What is known is that if you're lucky, or unlucky, enough to find a copy, you would be wise to tread lightly. Within every legend there is a grain of truth. This might be one time when it's best not to tempt fate.

Chapter 19:
Black Dogs

There are few who will argue the loyalty and trustworthiness of the domesticated dog. For millions of people, this most devoted of animals is as much a part of the family as any human could ever be. Perhaps this is why they appear in anecdotes as spirit guides tasked with leading souls to their ultimate destiny. These ghostly apparitions can be either a source of comfort at the time of death or the first of many terrors yet to come. The latter are known in the world of urban legends as "Black Dogs."

In Central and South America, El Cadejos are fabled spirits who roam the earth in the guise of dogs. These mystical beings can represent good or evil, depending upon the color of their thick coat of fur. It is a widely held belief that the black El Cadejo is an agent sent to do the devil's bidding.

These formidable beings are said to stalk the night; always on the prowl for victims. The dogs spend the hours from dusk until sunrise searching the back alleys and isolated roadways for stragglers who have lost their way. Those who have had a bit too much to drink and can't find their way home are also targeted by the hunters.

These otherworldly canines have been gifted the ability to know what exists in the recesses of the human mind. If someone is up to no good or has committed an unforgivable act, the dogs sense the bad blood and will act accordingly.

Once an El Cadejo has honed in on its prey, the beast makes no secret of its presence. The intended victim is suddenly aware that they are not alone as something they can't quite make out begins circling them. The game of cat and mouse continues until the dog has led its target to the brink of panic. It is then that the hunter makes its move.

Using the power of hypnosis, the animal stares deeply into the eyes of its victim. During this process, it is believed that the soul is extracted, leaving behind only a mindless shell. Its mission accomplished, the black dog returns to the shadows where it lies in wait for the next passerby.

While under the spell of this devilish creature, one is forced to do its bidding. A lifetime of servitude awaits those whose souls are not extracted outright. Freed from the spell, the party leaves with only a mild recollection of the incident. In the end, the reprieve is only temporary for once one is marked by the El Cadejo, their place in Hell has been reserved.

Although this unholy guide usually takes the form of a dog, it can also appear as a half- human/half-canine hybrid that walks upright on its hind legs. The manifestation of this creature is said to be accompanied by the sickening smell of rotten eggs. This pungent stench is reputed to be a sign that something demonic is nearby.

Wanderers who survive confrontations with the dogs claim that they suffer from memory loss and blackouts for the rest of their lives. Their personalities also undergo drastic, and sometimes frightening, transformations.

Those who live to tell the tale report that, following the encounters, they have uncontrollable urges to commit acts that they know are wrong. Some, unable to stop themselves, have followed through with their impulses. They only learn the details of their wrongdoing after the fact. For many of these pathetic souls, the fate they are handed is one worse than death.

As always, where there is darkness, there is also light. The white dog is the antithesis of its black counterpart. It is also lauded as the more powerful of the two. Created for the greater good, it assumes the role of protector for those who cannot look after themselves. It also thwarts the efforts of its devilish cousin whenever possible.

These loving guardians seek out the most innocent among us to keep out of harm's way; this usually consists of infants, children, and anyone else who cannot defend themselves. The dog also has a reputation for coming to the aid of weary travelers who are unaware of the sinister things that hide in the shadows.

White dogs, knowing that the black El Cadejo can be lurking around every corner, see to it that those passing through make it safely to their destination. That is, of course, if they are pure of heart. Those with less than noble intentions are left to fend for themselves.

There is only one scenario in which the white dog is rendered impotent. This occurs when the black dog is seen dragging a heavy chain. In this case, even the symbol of hope sent by God is powerless to intervene. This incarnation is said to be the devil on earth. It comes for only the most unsalvageable of souls and thus cannot be challenged.

In some areas of the Americas, the roles of the dogs are reversed. The white dog becomes the one to fear while the black guide acts as defender of the lost and downtrodden.

Both dogs are described as being larger than any domesticated canine known to man. Rather than bounding along as dogs are prone to do, they move with the elegance and grace of a deer.

They also sport cloven hooves instead of paws. This leads many to believe that these beings are not animals at all, but monstrosities that have assumed a form deemed more palatable to the human eye.

Stories of mystical creatures that are canine in appearance can be found in nearly every corner of the globe. In the United Kingdom, tales of malevolent black dogs have been around for centuries.

These hellhounds are believed to be omens of death and misfortune. With their glowing eyes and imposing stature, it is clear that they do not belong in this world. These ominous messengers tend to show up just before catastrophic events.

Mysterious black dogs have reportedly been sighted shortly before violent storms move in to wreak havoc on towns and villages. In centuries gone by, they were spotted milling about the sites where executions were scheduled to take place. Wherever death and destruction waited in the wings, so did the hellhounds.

The British black dogs are strictly nocturnal visitors that spend their days in places humans seldom go. Possessing the ability to shape-shift, they can mimic the appearance of any creature of their choosing. In a pack of dogs, they immediately assimilate. If they find themselves surrounded by people; that is the form they assume.

Hellhounds are thought to stay in the vicinity of a crossroads whenever possible. These areas exist on the cusp of this world and the next. They are a space between realms where the walls that separate the living from the dead are at their weakest point.

It is at a crossroads that spirits will most likely make contact with those they have left behind. Earthbound souls that are still undecided as to where their loyalties lie lurk near these entryways. Black dogs keep them company, all the while edging them towards a darker plane of existence.

In Swaledale, Yorkshire, a headless black dog is rumored to have laid claim to the Ivelet Bridge. For years, travelers to the area have reported hearing phantom barking as they were passing through. The animal sounds as though it is in distress, but no one dares to render aid, well-aware that anyone who sees it in the flesh is doomed to die before the end of the calendar year.

For those who lay eyes upon the horribly mutilated dog, it's all downhill from there. Over time, they lose the function of their limbs. As things progress, their ability to speak is also taken from them. No medical explanation can be found for the symptoms that effectively end the life they once knew.

It is said that to encounter the apparition of a headless dog is to keep company with a bad soul. These anomalies are forced to return to Earth in this hideous form as punishment for sins committed in a past life. This distasteful variety of spirit dog most often runs in packs. Anyone who crosses their path knows instantly that death is near.

The idea has been put forth that those who sell their souls to the devil are rewarded with the ability to assume the form of black dogs at sunset. In their new skin, they are free to roam the countryside, claiming victims at will. This notion dates back to the 15th century and continues today.

Christian churches had an unknowing hand in binding dogs to demonic forces. In olden days, some of the devout in Europe would bury a live dog under the stone foundation of their place of worship. This practice was intended to keep unsavory spirits and pagans at bay.

The belief was that the dog would rise at nightfall and guard the churchyard until morning light. Known as "Church Grims," these sacrificial dogs were required to possess only one essential attribute; they had to be black.

Some churches that were located near graveyards also let superstition get the better of them. As a way to ensure that no harm came to their parishioners, it was a long-standing tradition that the first man buried on the grounds would be eternally tasked with warding off the devil and his horde of demons each night after the sun went down.

Understandably, no one wanted the responsibility of fighting off the instruments of evil every night until the end of time. As a way around the issue, it was decided that a black dog would be interred prior to the first human burial. The dog's spirit would take on the monumental role of protector of the church and all its attendees. Eager to please, even in death, the animal sacrificed to save man did just that without a whimper of complaint. Or, at least, that is what they believed.

Winged black dogs resembling ravens also exist in the annals of lore. These menacing creatures allegedly descend from the night sky and soar over the homes of those who have been marked for death.

Legend has it that the flying dogs represented the souls of children who died without having been baptized. The loud cries said to emanate from the night sky when the winged creatures appeared have been likened to the wails of an infant.

As terrifying an image as that is, it is now believed that the nocturnal visitors were actually flocks of geese. Since these large birds often travel by night, they could easily be mistaken for something far more sinister. It is a bit of a stretch since their calls don't resemble a baby's cries in the slightest, but it is probably closer to reality than winged dogs.

Black dogs often get a bad rap, but there are times when they are assigned the role of saviors. For instance, stories have emerged over the years of hunters, in both Europe and the Americas, who claimed that they were rescued by enigmatic dogs after getting lost in the woods.

The accounts are strikingly similar as one after another, experienced outdoorsmen tell of getting turned around in the forest and losing their way. After wandering around aimlessly for hours, they find themselves being guided by a large black dog that appears out of nowhere. Once they reach a path that the hunter recognizes, the animal retreats into the thick brush, never to be seen again.

One of the most remarkable accounts of dogs putting themselves between an innocent victim and someone bent on doing them harm occurred in Buenos Aires, Argentina in 2013. The horrific ordeal began when a twelve-year old girl set out on her own to visit an aunt who lived nearby.

As the child navigated the city streets, a stranger suddenly grabbed her from behind and dragged her, kicking and screaming, into a back alley. Once he had her alone, the man attempted to sexually assault the terrified youngster.

The girl cried out for help, but her frantic pleas fell upon deaf ears. That is, until a pack of dogs barreled into the alley, making a beeline for the assailant. As the canine heroes threw themselves at the man, the girl jumped up and ran for safety.

None of the dogs made any attempt to chase the girl. They remained unified in their goal of subduing the man. The girl later stated that the dogs were nowhere to be seen in the minutes leading up to the attack. They had not been present on the street or in the alley. All the same, they showed up just when she needed them most.

Police investigating the scene shortly after the events took place could find no trace of the dogs. The man was also gone, leaving behind only droplets of blood. He has never been identified.

Buenos Aires, like most metropolitan areas, has an abundance of stray animals roaming its streets. The group of canines that saved the young girl from a violent attack set themselves apart from the rest with their selfless act.

Speculation loomed after the incident made national headlines that the dogs were something more than simply four-legged street urchins that happened to be at the right place at exactly the right time. This band of saviors had appeared out of nowhere with a single purpose: to stand between a child and the adult who wanted to hurt her.

It was noted that most street dogs are not treated with kindness by the people they encounter. Because of this, they tend to avoid human contact. This made it all the more remarkable that these vagabonds did not hesitate to put the life of an innocent above their own. Wherever the girl's protectors came from, it was there that they returned; their duty fulfilled.

In yet another instance, this one occurring in the Isle of Man, a mysterious dog may very well have saved the crew of a fishing boat from hazardous conditions that awaited them at sea. It all began when the schooner was preparing to set out from Peel Harbour on a night expedition. The waters were relatively calm as everyone boarded the boat. Everyone that is, except for the captain.

The crew paced impatiently throughout the night as they awaited the arrival of their leader. Left with no other choice, the exasperated fishermen abandoned their plans as daylight approached. They didn't know why at the time, but their captain had cost them a night's worth of fishing and thus, a hefty paycheck.

Just as dawn was breaking, a freak storm swept through that ravaged everything in its path. Any boat unfortunate enough to be away from port would most assuredly not escape the tempest's wrath. The crew of the fishing boat, who had been fuming earlier due to the aborted plans, were now grateful that they had escaped the worst of the storm. As a result, they lived to fish another day.

When the captain finally showed up, he informed his mates that he had tried several times during the night to join them. He explained that his progress had been impeded by a dog that refused to let him on the dock that led to the vessel.

The captain described the animal as having been massive in size and solid black in color. It had also possessed eyes that glowed red in the dim light. He remarked that he had never seen the dog before that evening. Nevertheless, it had stayed with him for hours, blocking any attempts he made to access the area where the boat was docked.

Realizing that he could not compete with the remarkably resolute dog, the captain eventually gave up and left the pier. Once the storm had passed, the dog vanished and was never seen again. The fishermen couldn't explain the events that had occurred that night. All they knew was that a black dog had saved them from almost certain ruin, and possibly an unplanned burial at sea.

It is possible that some of the dogs that witnesses describe are either English Mastiffs or Newfoundlands. Mastiffs can reach upwards of two hundred pounds and stand three feet tall. Likewise, Newfoundlands have roughly the same characteristics, sometimes measuring up to six feet in length from nose to tail.

Some accounts of black dogs, whether they are the good or evil variety, have undoubtedly been exaggerated with each telling. Others, however, are not easily explained away. Perhaps the truth lies somewhere in the hazy grey area that exists between the world of certainties and the land of possibilities.

Chapter 20:
The Show Must Go On

The following urban legend is another involving our four-legged friends. The fantastic beasts that live and breathe in this tale are much larger and nearly impossible to ignore. It is in this corner of lore that the infamous ghost elephants are said to reside.

Forest Park, Illinois is the site of a cemetery reserved for circus performers who have moved on to that Big Top in the sky. Christened "Showman's Rest," the land was acquired in 1918 by the Showman's League of America. Their intention was to provide a dignified final stop for those who had devoted their lives to the road.

Sadly, for some, that time would come much sooner than anyone could have foreseen. A tragic train crash later the same year claimed the lives of nearly a hundred entertainers who would become the first to be interred in the newly established cemetery. Dozens of animals were also lost in the accident.

The horrific events unfolded when a train carrying members of the Hagenbeck-Wallace Circus was hit by a Michigan Central Railroad car while traveling from Detroit to Chicago. The performers' train had been stopped on the tracks near the town of Hammond, Indiana while undergoing minor repairs. As a safety measure, they had activated warning lights that would alert oncoming locomotives to proceed with extreme caution.

It was in the early hours of June 22 that the circus train was rear-ended. The crash ignited a fire that spread rapidly through the wooden cars. Many of those who survived the initial impact were unable to escape the inferno. By the time that help arrived, it was too little, too late.

An investigation would later determine that the collision had been the direct result of the conductor of the other train having fallen asleep at the controls. He had neither seen nor heard the warnings put in place by those aboard the circus train.

The damage had been so devastating that many of the bodies could not be identified. Their mangled remains were buried in the grounds of Showman's Rest underneath markers that read simply "Unidentified Male or Female."

Survivors were left to pick up the pieces of their shattered lives. Even as the process of grieving and recovery were underway, so were plans to continue with the scheduled shows. With help from other circus' that donated borrowed equipment as well as performers, Hagenbeck-Wallace Circus carried on as best it could.

Not long after the fallen artists had been laid to rest, local residents reported hearing what sounded like elephants trumpeting in the area after nightfall. It was true that elephants had died alongside their handlers in the crash, but none had been buried in Showman's Rest.

The smaller of the non-human victims were hauled away, leaving only the elephant carcasses behind. Too large to move, the remains of the once majestic creatures were left to rot until time and the elements removed the last traces of their existence.

At Showman's Rest, five granite elephants stand watch over the graves of those who perished in the train wreck. Their heads bowed low in mourning; they are the vision of eternal sadness. The league that commissioned the statues knew well that no other creature would convey the sense of loss as effectively as these sorrowful giants.

It has been theorized that the sounds sometimes carried on the night air are those of the circus animals whose lives were claimed in the crash and subsequent fire. Although the accident occurred in another state, far away from the cemetery, some believe that the elephants remain connected to their human handlers in death, just as they were in life.

Given that the elephants had spent years living the lives of showman, something they were never meant to do, it makes some sense that they would have lost their true identities over time. With no memories of their prior lives, perhaps they clung to the only thing they knew: life inside the ring.

With the lights dimmed and no audiences to appease, the ghost elephants are said to herald their presence by bellowing as darkness envelops the world around them. Night after night, they announce to all within earshot that they are still around, at least as much as they can be.

No zoos or sanctuaries are located in the area of Showman's Rest. There are no wildlife reserves to be found. What explanation can there be for dozens of people coming forward to assert that they have heard the unmistakable calls of elephants coming from Showman's Rest? The answer, as unlikely as it may seem, could be that they are eavesdropping on events of the past as they play out in a place where only those who have captivated throngs of people are welcome.

It is not uncommon for people to see only what they want to see when it comes to that which exists outside of their comfort zone. Still, it isn't a bad thing to hope, in some way, that the elephants that lost their lives over a hundred years ago have stayed loyal to their fellow entertainers. Perhaps the performer's credo, "The Show Must Go On" applies to all who have stood in the spotlight, whether they did so on two legs or four.

Chapter 21:
Little Green Men

We've all heard stories of little green men that supposedly show up in rural areas and scare the daylights out of residents before returning to wherever it is they call home. What most of us don't know is that these visitors, along with the term commonly used to describe them, sprang from a terrifying real-life encounter.

Twenty miles from the Tennessee border sits the sleepy area of Kelly-Hopkinsville Kentucky. In 1955, this peaceful community would be rocked to its foundation one late August night when the Sutton family barged into the Hopkinsville police station with a story that would be remembered for decades to come.

The five adults and seven children would go on to insist that they had been driven from their farmhouse by a band of "little grey men" that had disembarked from a flying saucer that landed on their property.

Armed with shotguns, the clan had barricaded themselves inside as all-out war was waged against them. They described their aggressors as being two to three feet tall with overly large eyes. Dressed in dark attire that helped to camouflage them in the night, the tiny beings were unarmed, but fearless.

The puzzled officers who were trying to get up to speed, asked the family to backtrack and tell them what happened from the beginning. Billy Ray Taylor related that he had stepped outside after dinner to digest and take in the night air. In short order, he rushed into the house with a story that even his closest kin did not believe.

Billy Ray breathlessly recounted that he had just witnessed a large, metal object in the shape of a dinner plate hovering in the sky above the farmhouse. Billy Ray became agitated as his relatives laughed off the outlandish claims. Even though no one believed him, he knew that something was going on that was only going to get worse as the evening progressed.

Billy Ray paced the floor for several minutes, trying to figure out what to do next. After some time went by, he asked Elmer Sutton, whose mother Glennie owned the property, to accompany him outside to take a look at the craft for himself. Confident that there would be nothing to see, Elmer agreed to the request.

The men walked to the spot where Billy Ray claimed to have seen the flying saucer. Elmer was not surprised to find that there was no sign of anything in the sky other than the moon and stars.

As they were making their way back to the house, a glowing figure emerged from the adjoining woods. In what they assumed at first to be a gesture of goodwill, the being raised its hands in the air as it approached.

For a moment, the men stood watching in disbelief. When the strange interloper was close enough for them to get a good luck at what they were facing, they knew that its intentions were anything but pure.

Billy Ray and Elmer ran for the safety of the house, all the while yelling for the other family members to stay inside. As Glennie herded the children into a bedroom, the men of the house armed themselves for a battle they felt sure was coming.

They took up positions at the doors and windows ready to ward off anyone or anything that tried to cross the thresholds. Even as they observed the drama unfolding around them, some of the family members still thought that this frenzy of activity was part of an elaborate joke.

Glennie took her son aside and told him, point blank, that if this was some sort of game he needed to end it. Elmer assured her that the situation was deadly serious. When she asked him to tell her what he had seen in the yard, he informed her that she was better off not knowing.

After speaking with Elmer, Glennie's doubts were put to rest. She could always tell when her son wasn't being truthful. What she saw in his eyes and demeanor that night convinced her that he was not playing around. In the next moment, she grabbed a weapon and took her place beside the men.

As the family lay in wait, a lone figure appeared from out of the darkness and slowly approached the front door. Glennie let out a startled scream before she could stop herself. In a panic, Billy Ray fired through the door at the figure on the other side.

The would-be intruder fled into the woods at the sound of the gunshot. As they peered into the night, the family knew immediately that their troubles were far from over. From all around them, they could see dozens of eyes glowing in the surrounding trees.

As the night progressed, many of those reflective eyes would appear just outside of the windows. When this happened, someone would shoot at whatever was observing them through the glass. Glennie's other son C.J. shot at one of the creatures, sending it tumbling backwards onto the ground. It then jumped to its feet and took off running for the woods.

At some point, Glennie took to her knees in prayer. She believed that the things laying siege to her home were hellish creatures sent by the devil himself. The devoutly religious woman had no other explanation for the nightmare that she and her family were now facing.

The standoff lasted for over four hours. Sometime during the night, the things that were terrorizing the farmhouse suddenly vacated without warning. Once they sensed that the coast was clear, Glennie and her family high-tailed it to the police station.

Local law enforcement didn't know what to make of the story. They didn't believe for a second that aliens, goblins or any other entity had attacked the Sutton clan. That being said, they could tell by looking at the bedraggled individuals standing before them that they had experienced some kind of trauma.

With the goal of putting the matter to rest once and for all, the officers agreed to accompany the family to their home to get to the bottom of what happened. Upon their arrival, they noted that several windows had been shot out. The front door also sported a hole, courtesy of a shotgun blast.

What was conspicuously absent from the scene was any sign that the barrage of gunfire had made contact with the intended targets. No blood could be found anywhere, nor were there any bodies lying about.

What the investigators did find was copious amounts of a gooey substance they could not identify. The glowing fluorescent liquid was spattered about the property. Unfortunately, no samples were taken at the time and the evidence was washed away with the first rain shower.

Officers separated the family members and questioned them individually. Each told remarkably similar stories. Not one of them faltered or wavered from their account that they had been attacked by non-human beings.

Nothing much came of the inquiry. An unwanted aspect of their having told their story to authorities was that the account made headlines in the local newspaper. Soon, busybodies and curiosity seekers descended upon the already traumatized family. Everyone wanted to know more about the creatures that had been dubbed the "Kelly Green Men" by some; the "Kelly Green Goblins" by others.

Glennie and her relatives were ridiculed by people they had once considered friends. To add to their indignity, assertions were made that the adults had been drinking heavily on the night of the alleged incident. The glowing invaders were assumed by most to have been alcohol-induced hallucinations.

Anyone who was actually acquainted with Glennie knew that she was a teetotaler. She also forbade anyone else to consume liquor in her home. The much-maligned woman assured all who cared to listen that she and her family had been sober and in control of their faculties on the night in question. She also stressed that officers had searched the house and found no trace of booze on the premises.

One positive did emerge from all of the negative publicity when a neighbor of Glennie's came forward with a story that bolstered that of the beleaguered family.

The man reported that at roughly the same time that the Sutton property was being invaded, he had noticed mysterious lights coming from the woods around the farmhouse. Thinking that his neighbors were searching the forest with flashlights, perhaps for escaped livestock, he didn't give the sight much thought.

He also revealed that he had heard several gunshots throughout the night. Again, he assumed that it had something to do with missing or perhaps pilfered farm animals. It was only after he read the newspaper accounts that he realized he might have caught a glimpse into their ordeal as it was occurring.

After putting up with a steady stream of gawkers and reporters, Glennie had finally had enough. She eventually put the house she had lived in for decades up for sale. She no longer wanted anything to do with the place that had brought her only joy, that is, until the night it was targeted by green goblins.

The creatures that attacked the farm in 1955 were never seen again after that night. Speculation abounded as to the identity of the culprits, if they existed at all. Great horned owls were thought by many to be the most likely cause of the disturbances experienced by the Suttons.'

These night predators possess the large eyes described by the witnesses. They can grow to heights of over two feet tall, which would make them about the size of the creatures the family claimed waged war on their home.

This theory does not take into account Billy Ray's claim that he saw a large disc flying over the property. Nor does it address the recollections of both Billy Ray and Elmer that the first figure they encountered had held its arms in the air. Even in the moonlight, it is unlikely that they would have mistaken a four-foot wingspan for raised limbs.

It is also telling that no blood or wounded owls were found at the scene. The men who got off shots that night would tell investigators that they were certain they had made contact with at least some of their intended targets. If the assailants were indeed owls, how they escaped unscathed remains a mystery.

Why owls would have been so bold as to approach a houseful of people is also an aspect of the story that gives one pause. Predatory birds hunting small animals in the dead of night is to be expected; those same creatures refusing to back down from humans, even as gunfire erupts all around them is a stretch, to say the least.

It is worth noting that a meteor shower took place on the same night as the alleged attack. Others in the area reported seeing strange lights in the sky that were later attributed to the phenomenon.

The Suttons' story would leave a lasting impression on all those who heard it. Director Steven Spielberg was said to have used aspects of their account as inspiration for his film *Close Encounters of the Third Kind*.

As the incredible tale spread from one person to another, the hue of the invaders was mistakenly changed from grey to green. From that time on, "little green men" from space became a staple of science fiction worldwide.

Whether the Sutton family waged battle against aliens, goblins, imps or some other as-yet unidentified beings, no one will ever know for certain. It is undeniable that something unusual took place at the farmhouse on that night long ago. What it was, and who was responsible spawned an urban legend that has only grown over time.

Chapter 22:
100 Steps Cemetery

There are few places more frightening than graveyards. During the day, they are quiet areas, sometimes covered in flowers, where those who have passed on rest in eternal peace. At nightfall, however, they take on an entirely different persona; one where creatures banished from this plane reappear until the sun drives them back into the abyss.

As we all know, these events don't really happen. There is nothing present in the dark that isn't there in the light. This old adage might be true, but try telling that to the people who have visited a 19th century graveyard where death is supposedly foretold and nothing is as it seems.

Carpenter's Cemetery in Cloverland, Indiana has been around for well over a hundred years. Sometime in the early 1980s, rumors began to swirl that the old graveyard held a power that was as intriguing as it was terrifying.

It was said that those who wished to glimpse a preview of their own death could do so by climbing the stairs located near the entrance of the cemetery. Crumbling with time, some of the steps were barely usable while others were missing altogether. For those who would do anything to watch their future fate unfold, the precarious ascent was worth the risk.

There were strict rules that had to be adhered to in order to achieve the desired results. The first of these was that the participant had to begin their climb as the clock struck twelve. On their way up, they had to count every step, being careful not to miss one or lose their place. To be off by even a single number was to dash all hope of encountering the specter that was said to be waiting at the top of the stairs. It was also imperative that every number be shouted out loud for all to hear, most importantly, the holder of the future who was waiting at the end of the climb.

Some gave up as nerves overtook them. The ones who completed the task found themselves face-to-face with a shrouded figure said to be the spirit of the graveyard's first undertaker. The dark entity would then pass his arm in front of the eyes of whoever stood before him. In those moments, the person saw his or her own death reflected in real time.

His obligation met, the undertaker vanished as the person who had just seen the future turned and made their way back down the stairs. This is where things got tricky. On the descent, the person had to, again, count every step. It was of the utmost importance at that stage of the game that no mistakes were made.

When the person reached the last step, the number had to be the same as the count going up. If the numbers were off, the vision would come to pass. If they were an exact match, the undertaker's prediction would be rendered null and void.

As it happened, the cards were stacked in the cemetery's favor all along. In the pitch darkness, unaided by artificial light, the night played tricks on the already anxious subject. Since the steps were in dire shape, it was nearly impossible to keep an accurate count; a fact well-known to the undertaker.

Most people who made the sojourn knew in advance that if they didn't count a hundred steps on the way up, their efforts would be for naught. This prompted many an adventurous soul to fudge the numbers. For his part, the specter could not be fooled. If someone tried to deceive him, they were met with empty space when they reached the top.

There is no shortage of people who like to take shortcuts in life and this was no exception. Scofflaws who bypassed the stairs, but still expected to be rewarded, were in for a rude awakening. To commit this act of disrespect was to be marked with the devil's handprint.

The offending brand would appear on either the back or chest of anyone who didn't follow the rules. The print would remain for several days as a reminder of their misdeed. During this time, the person was aware every moment of the day that they had been touched by evil. The burning pain they endured made sure of it.

This story was recounted in past tense for a reason. In recent years, the old stairway to the sky was completely replaced. Now, instead of a hundred steps, there are only sixty. The keepers of the cemetery have also become more diligent in their efforts to keep trespassers out once the gates are closed for the night. These changes have not, however, completely put an end to speculation that there is more to Carpenter's Cemetery than meets the eye.

In spite of the new construction, there are still those who sneak in to see if the legend is real. One man who climbed the stairs claimed that his cell phone malfunctioned as he was making his way to the top. He was also overcome by an eerie feeling so unsettling that it forced him to abandon his plan and return to the safety of the ground below.

No one knows for sure how the cemetery gained its spooky reputation. One possible factor could be its location. The property sits in the Wabash Valley, an area that has a penchant for paranormal activity.

Hell's Gate is located in the valley, not far from Carpenter's Cemetery. The antiquated viaduct was once the site of a train derailment that is said to have resulted in dozens of casualties. The ghosts of those who died are believed to still haunt the area where they drew their last breaths.

A one-lane tunnel beneath the span is reputed to be swarming with these trapped spirits. It is rumored that they can be summoned to appear by those who perform a short, but effective ritual. Drivers must enter the tunnel, stopping at the halfway point. They have to then flash their headlights three times in quick succession. Once this is accomplished, they must exit the tunnel, turn around and re-enter from the opposite side.

This time, they have to stop and cut the engine. After a ten minute wait, something will begin knocking on the windows. Blood soon oozes from the walls and runs down onto the pavement. If the driver's name appears in the gooey liquid, they will not live to see the sunrise.

A haunted house in nearby Bellmore also marked the area as a supernatural stomping ground. The home, built shortly after the end of the Civil War, was plagued by strange occurrences right from the start.

During construction, a newly erected chimney fell to the ground overnight. Tools would turn up missing only to be found in an area where they had never been used.

Once the house was built and a family moved in, things only got worse. One night, every article of the family's clothing disappeared from the home. The next morning, the trees in the yard were adorned with the missing wardrobe items.

The incident might have been dismissed as a prank if not for the fact that much of the clothing was found clinging to branches high up in the treetops. It would have been impossible for anyone to have climbed the trees since the limbs were deemed too thin and brittle to withstand the weight of anything heavier than a squirrel or other small mammal.

It was also telling that the clothes were found wrapped tightly around every visible part of the trees as if each one had been meticulously placed. However the feat had been accomplished, it was determined that it had not been the work of human hands.

These are just a few examples offered to lend credence to the theory that the Wabash Valley has close ties to the spirit world. Whether it is situated near a portal to another dimension or is simply an area with more than its fair share of overactive imaginations is anyone's guess. Either way, 100 Steps Cemetery continues to attract those who believe there is something to the story. Thanks to them, the legend lives on.

Chapter 23:
The Bunny Man

Fairfax County, Virginia was the setting for a terrifying bit of lore that made the rounds in the 1970s. This one involved a killer dressed in a bunny outfit who randomly attacked strangers with a hatchet or other sharp implement. The real story did not stray far from this narrative.

The first of two incidents that put the citizens of Burke, Virginia on edge occurred in October of 1970. It began when U.S. Air Force Academy Cadet Robert Bennett and his girlfriend set out one evening to pay a visit to the home of a relative.

When the couple pulled into the driveway of the uncle's house on Guinea Road, they were immediately accosted by an imposing figure who emerged from out of the shadows. Within seconds, the man had swung an object towards the car, smashing the front passenger side window. The horrified occupants of the vehicle shielded themselves as they were showered with broken glass.

As the thoroughly shaken pair sat frozen to their seats, the attacker railed at them for trespassing. Bennett knew that the man was in the wrong since his uncle owned the land. Ironically, the only one who had no business being on the property was the accuser. Sensing that arguing with the obviously unhinged man would do more harm than good, Bennett listened in silence as threats were hurled at both him and his girlfriend.

After he had said his peace, the aggressor abruptly turned tail and disappeared into the night. Bennett drove straight to the nearest police station to report the ordeal. Once there, the victims related the incident as best they could.

Neither of them had gotten a good look at the man, but they both noted that he was tall and dressed completely in white. At some point, one of them supposedly mentioned that they thought he had been dressed in a rabbit costume.

The couple differed in their recollections of what the crazed man had worn on his head. Bennett allegedly stated that the finishing touch to the outfit had been a large, cone-shaped hat similar to the ones worn in religious ceremonies. His girlfriend insisted that the accessory had not been a hat at all, but rather, bunny ears.

Although, both of them claimed to have seen the man's face illuminated by nearby streetlamps, neither could describe his features. For reasons they couldn't explain, details of his appearance had been wiped from their memories.

Investigators who processed the car found a hatchet lying nearby. It was presumed that the tool had been used by the "Bunny Man" to break the window. No other evidence was found that would prove to be of any use in identifying the perpetrator. Nothing came of the report and no arrests were ever made.

Ten days later, on October 29, a night watchman named Paul Phillips would have his own run-in with the lunatic of Guinea Road. While working security at a building site, he noticed a man loitering on the porch of a house that was in the finishing stages of construction.

As Phillips approached the trespasser, he knew immediately that he was about to earn his money. He could see that the man was not only dressed head-to-toe in an oversized bunny suit, but that he was also wielding an axe.

Before the stunned guard could say a word, the man lifted the axe and began hacking away at the posts on either side of the porch. As he swung the tool, he warned Phillips that he would get a taste of the same if he didn't leave the property at once.

Realizing that his flashlight was no match for an axe, Phillips retreated. He reported the incident as quickly as possible, but the man had vacated by the time law enforcement officials arrived. Just as in the previous encounter, no useful evidence was found the case went nowhere.

Over the span of the next few weeks, some fifty residents claimed to have been waylaid by a hostile man wearing a bunny suit. The unpleasant interactions usually began with people out minding their own business who suddenly found themselves being accused of trespassing by a larger-than-life, exceedingly angry rabbit. After hearing him out, they would remove themselves from the situation as quickly as possible.

Curiously, the only aspect of the stories that varied was the color of the costume the man had worn. In the Bennett episode, it had been white. Phillips described the garment as having been multi-colored. It was assumed that the perpetrator had as many bunny suits as he did complaints against those he viewed as interlopers.

Police investigated as best they could, but found themselves hitting brick walls time and again. Since no one could describe the man's face, they had little to go on. Dressed in street attire, he would have been unrecognizable, even to his multitude of victims.

The story was picked up by the media in nearby Washington, D.C. and soon spread like wildfire. Unsubstantiated claims began to circulate that the "Bunny Man" was stealing pets and consuming them on the spot. As a precaution, worried animal lovers kept watchful eyes on their cats and dogs just in case a bloodthirsty killer really was on the loose.

As the story grew, some armchair sleuths thought that they had figured out the identity of the culprit. It seemed that, in 1904, a local eccentric named Douglas Grifon had murdered his entire family with an axe. Brought to trial, the man was declared criminally insane. Instead of being sent to prison, he had been committed to a mental institution in Clifton, Virginia.

When the facility was forced to shut down ten years later, the residents were doled out to other institutions. During one of these transports, the bus crashed, killing several of the staff members and inmates on board.

In the aftermath of the accident, a handful of the passengers who had not been seriously injured escaped into the night. As fate would have it, the axe murderer had been one of the lucky ones who made a dash for freedom.

In the days following the incident, all of the escapees were rounded up and placed in the care of the state. All, that is, except for Grifon. A county-wide alert was issued, but no sign of the notorious family killer was ever found. He did, however, make his presence known.

It wasn't long before residents started noticing the carcasses of dead rabbits littering their yards. The tiny creatures were often found skinned and completely drained of blood. A multitude of theories were offered up as to what kind of animal was responsible for the senseless slaughter, but none of them explained the condition of the bodies.

The Colchester Road Bridge was rumored to be a favorite haunt of the creature dubbed the "Bunny Man." His presence there was said to be the result of Grifon's having been struck by a train only moments after fleeing the scene of the bus crash. Apparently, the reason that the axe murderer hadn't been captured was that he had been dead all along.

It is said that the tunnel beneath the bridge is inhabited by a sinister being that leaves the mutilated bodies of rabbits behind as its calling card. Even today, people claim to occasionally find their tiny, decimated forms hanging from the trees that abut the railway bridge.

The legend of the lunatic who lives inside the one-lane tunnel and feasts on raw rabbits was linked, decades later to the "Bunny Man" encounters of the 1970s. The connection is questionable, mainly due to the fact that no one seems to be able to prove definitively that Douglas Grifon, axe murderer, ever existed.

Robert Bennett and his girlfriend (now wife) gave an interview several years after their ordeal in which they relived the horrifying events of the night they were attacked. Neither of them recalled saying that the man had been dressed in a bunny suit.

As with many stories that take on lives of their own, that tidbit might have been added later as the tale spread via word-of-mouth. It is also possible that the couple had chosen to forget as much about that night as they could, which would be completely understandable.

One memory that stayed with Bennett's wife over the years was that of combing pieces of glass out of her hair in the days following the attack. She had also sustained cuts to her face as the window exploded beside her. The tiny scars left behind were a constant reminder of the encounter.

The knowledge that the man responsible was never apprehended weighed heavily on the Bennetts for a long time. Eventually, they came to terms with the realization that closure would not be forthcoming.

Who, or what, the "Bunny Man" truly was will probably never be known. It could be that he was simply a grouchy resident of Guinea Road who took it upon himself to drive away anyone he felt was invading his territory. A coward at heart, perhaps donning a costume was his way of ensuring that he would not be held accountable for his actions.

There are still those who believe that the "Bunny Man" of Guinea Road and the infamous Douglas Grifon are one and the same. It is doubtful, but in this place of lore where nothing is as it seems, anything is possible.

Chapter 24:
Hider in the House

We would all like to think that there is no place safer in the world than our own humble abode. The "Stranger in the House" urban legend flies in the face of that belief. Although there are several variations of this tale, the basic premise is the same.

The story normally begins in a quiet town where residents sleep peacefully at night; secure in the knowledge that bad things only happen to city folk or people who put themselves in harm's way. Little do they know that someone is close by; hiding in plain sight.

In a nutshell, a housebreaker finds the perfect place to call his own. The only trouble is that someone is already living there, but he doesn't let that get in his way. He moves in and makes himself at home, coming and going when no one else is around.

Sometime along the way, the squatter who has secreted himself away in the attic or crawlspace is found out, either by accident or because he tires of the ruse. A confrontation ensues which usually ends with someone in a pool of blood. Sadly, in these tales, that someone is the homeowner.

As the saga comes to a close, the one who has kept his presence a well-guarded secret for months, or sometimes years, retreats to his hideaway where he stays until someone else moves in, at which point the cycle begins again. With each new occupant, he ups his game, always winning when all is said and done.

Common sense dictates that such a ridiculous series of events would be impossible. No intelligent person could carry on with their life, day in and day out, completely unaware that they had an intruder living in their home. As you are about to see, what makes sense and reality aren't always the same thing.

One of the first documented cases of just such an occurrence took place in Denver, Colorado in 1941. The circumstances were so unique that they helped to spawn an eerie tale of lore that would become the basis of horror films for years to come.

Philip Peters lived a life to be proud of. Seventy-three years of age at the time, he had kept his head low for most of his life. He had worked hard, married his childhood sweetheart and proved himself to be a reliable friend and neighbor. It would be exactly that good nature that would seal his fate.

That September, Peters' ailing wife had been admitted to a local hospital. Always the devoted husband, he had spent most of his time by her side during her recovery. Returning home each day after visiting hours ended; he would have a bite of dinner before bathing and grabbing a few hours of sleep. In the morning, he would wake and do it all again.

Theodore Edward Coneys had been a friend of Peters' on and off for years. The two men couldn't have been more different, but they got along in their own way. Peters felt a bit sorry for the other man who never seemed to catch a break. Coneys, on the other hand, watched his friend's success with a resentment that would only grow over time.

Coneys, unlike Philip Peters, had not prospered in life. Unable to find a path that suited him, he had lived hand-to-mouth for as long as he could remember. Soup kitchens and sleeping outdoors would become all-too familiar to the aging ne'er do well.

In an unfortunate bit of timing, Coneys found himself once again facing the prospect of homelessness at the same time that Peters' wife was in the hospital. Deciding to pay his old friend a visit, Coneys showed up on a day when no one was home. He saw it as a perfect opportunity to get what he had always wanted, a chance to live the life of Philip Peters.

Coneys let himself in that day and never left. After having a look around the house, the hard feelings he harbored towards Peters only intensified. There was no denying that his friend had certainly done well for himself. Coneys decided then and there that it was time for a change.

A plan began to take shape as he memorized the layout of the interior. He made up his mind that the attic would provide him the shelter he needed, at least until more suitable accommodations became available.

Once he settled in, Coneys couldn't believe his good fortune. With the owners gone most of the day; he had run of the house. As soon as Peters left in the morning, Coneys would come down to the kitchen and prepare breakfast. He would then clean up and lounge around the home for hours on end. In no time at all, he had his oblivious host's schedule down pat. Things were almost too easy. All the same, Coneys knew that the arrangement couldn't go on forever.

One morning, over a month into his stay, Coneys heard the front door close signaling that the coast was clear. He made his way downstairs and proceeded to whip up a meal, as he had done every day since he moved in.

What Coneys didn't know was that Peters had opened the door briefly, but had turned around when he realized that he needed to retrieve something from his bedroom. In the harrowing moments that followed, the two men faced each other for the first time in ten years.

So much time had passed since their last meeting that Peters didn't even recognize the man standing in his kitchen. Seizing the moment, Coneys began mercilessly beating the bewildered homeowner. Peters would die that morning at the hands of Coneys, never knowing that they had been living under the same roof for several weeks.

After the deed was done, Coneys went back up to the attic like nothing had happened. As the day progressed, he decided to take advantage of his newfound freedom. Thanks to the violent turn of events, he had the place all to himself with no fear of being found out. At last, he was the man of the house.

Several days went by before anyone noticed that something was wrong. Hospital staff began questioning why Peters' visits had suddenly stopped. They had all seen his unwavering commitment to his wife and couldn't imagine that anything would keep him from her.

Neighbors also took note of his absence. A familiar presence around town, it was out of character for him to just up and disappear. Worried friends took it upon themselves to perform a welfare check. What they found was far worse than any of them had imagined.

After receiving no answer to their persistent knocks on the front door, the group tried the knob. Finding that it was unlocked, they entered the residence. They called out to Peters, but received no response.

The silence in the house was deafening as they made their way into the kitchen. It was there, lying in a pool of congealed blood, that they found the decaying corpse of Philip Peters. The police were called in immediately and an investigation was soon underway.

Authorities could find no signs of a break-in which indicated to them that the victim had let his killer into the home willingly. Nothing appeared to have been disturbed, ruling out burglary as a motive. With no witnesses and no suspects in mind, the case was filed away until such a time when new evidence could be brought to light.

Mrs. Peters was released from the hospital shortly after the discovery of her husband's body. With no place else to go, she moved back into the home they had shared. Still recovering from her ailments, she hired a housekeeper to help her until she could get back on her feet. The woman would be the first of what would turn out to be a revolving door of aides.

One after another, the helpers tasked with the care of Mrs. Peters fell to the wayside. Some left without explanation while others quit after only a few days, declaring that they feared there was a ghost on the premises.

Left without anyone to render assistance, the elderly woman moved in with her son and his family. The decision, made out of necessity, probably saved her life.

Coneys had been in the house the entire time. It was he who had spooked the staff. He had been careful to frighten them away while still maintaining his anonymity. Once again, he had the place to himself. What Coneys didn't realize was that all good things eventually come to an end.

Things began to unravel when eagle-eyed neighbors noticed lights on inside the supposedly vacant house. When police were notified, they set up surveillance in the area. One evening, in the summer of 1942, they finally hit the jackpot when one of them saw a man peering out at them from behind a curtain in the Peters' home.

Forcing their way into the house, the officers apprehended Coneys as he attempted to flee to his roost in the attic. It was the one area of the home that had not been searched at the time of Philip Peters' murder. The reason given at the time was that the opening into the room was too small for an adult to fit through. After seeing Coneys in the flesh, his diminutive size surprised investigators. Small in stature, but as strong as any man twice his size, the killer had found the perfect hiding place.

Coneys was tried and convicted of the brutal murder of Philip Peters. He died in prison in 1967 while serving out his life sentence. The legacy he left behind was one not many would wish to claim.

The incidence of people stowing away in the residences of others is rare, but it does occur more often than one would think. There have been numerous accounts of home invaders found hiding in walls, attics, crawlspaces, cellars and basements. Sometimes, they are acquaintances of the homeowners, sometimes not.

In most cases, these unwanted guests leave on their own when they sense that their cover is about to be blown. When they are discovered, it is often completely by accident. Fortunately, the confrontations that inevitably follow don't usually end as horribly as that of Philip Peters and Theodore Coneys.

For those who have experienced these unfathomable events, the scars run long and deep. Besides the clear violation of privacy, the victims also suffer a loss of innocence. After what they have gone through, they can never again rest in the knowledge that they are safe at home.

Chapter 25:
Water Babies

Urban legends aren't confined to any specific part of the world, nor do they only take place on land. Sometimes, these cautionary tales spring from rivers, lakes and oceans. Such is the case with the restless souls known as "Water Babies."

Idaho's famed Snake River is said to be home to a spawn of creatures that dwell deep beneath the surface. Possessing an appetite for vengeance, as well as a taste for fresh meat, these ferocious predators take the form of small children in order to lull their intended victims into a false state of well-being.

The Water Babies are skilled hunters; adept at capturing prey. When they sense the presence of a hapless fisherman or hiker, they emit the pitiful cries of an infant. The good-hearted passerby will naturally dive into the river in search of the child who is obviously in distress, although not yet visible to the eye.

Once the quarry has taken the bait, the masquerade is over. The horrified victim realizes as they are being pulled under the surface that they have made a terrible mistake. As they enter the icy depths, the last thing they see is something resembling a human child that has been modified with gills, fins and sharp teeth ideal for tearing through flesh.

The story behind this gruesome legend dates back to 1805 when the area surrounding the river was inhabited by the Shoshone and Bannock Native American tribes. It was a time of upheaval, due in part to the arrival of colonists passing through on their way west in search of a better life.

The steady flow of settlers depleted the natural resources more rapidly than anyone could have predicted. The influx resulted in a food shortage that devastated the native people. It was rumored that desperate parents, unable to feed their families, were forced to cull their offspring.

The loathsome tale recounts that, with more hungry mouths than food, newborn infants were taken to the river and drowned. The action, as unfathomable as it seems, was deemed a kinder option than subjecting the babies to slow deaths by starvation. These tiny forms, doomed from birth, were sacrificed so that their siblings could live.

As days turned into weeks and then years, life improved in the valley. It wasn't until a mysterious rash of drownings hit the area that denizens began to wonder if the Snake River was cursed.

Several people who had been drawn to the water's edge claimed that they had been enticed to enter the river by a child's cries for help. At the last minute, a primal instinct had kicked in and prevented them from offering assistance.

Some didn't see the source of the cries, but those who did would never forget the thing they laid eyes upon. Those witnesses described a fish-like creature with the features of a young child. They could tell by its behavior that the monstrosity was trying with all its might to make its way to land. Fortunately, something prevented it from leaving the water, presumably, the lack of legs.

Many who either heard the stories or claimed to have seen the oddities for themselves, theorized that the mutated beings were the souls of the babies who were drowned decades earlier during the time of famine.

It was believed that these forlorn spirits, robbed of their chance to live, had become one with the water instead of moving on. As time passed, they developed the characteristics of aquatic life in order to survive. With the addition of gills, they were able to breathe underneath the water, coming to the surface only when the desire to hunt became greater than the need to remain hidden.

Filled with resentment for having been sacrificed to the river, the babies made it their mission to exact revenge on all those who walked on land. They learned quickly that humans could be easily manipulated. Willing to throw caution to the wind to answer the cries of a child in danger, these victims were ripe for the picking. Once they fell for the ruse and dove into the water, they were held under until they gasped their last breath.

Today, Massacre Rocks State Park, so named for the ambushes that occurred there during covered wagon days, is a part of history that will never be forgotten. It is also the area in which the Water Babies are said to dwell.

The beauty and serenity of Snake River are believed to mask something sinister that lies in wait below the water. There is no denying that the thousand mile stretch that runs from Wyoming to Washington State has been the site of countless hardships over the centuries. Who is to say what lurks in the depths of this massive waterway?

It is likely that tales of ferocious Water Babies were something made up by cautious parents as a way of preventing their adventurous children from getting too close to the river's edge and possibly falling in. What better way to ensure their safety than with the threat of flesh-eating mutants?

Whether or not the stories contain a grain of truth is hard to say. Transmogrified fish and other marine life are certainly a real occurrence. Perhaps, someplace between the legend of the Water Babies and the reality of creatures that have transitioned into beings not yet recognized by science, lies the truth.

Chapter 26:
The Dark Watchers

The Santa Lucia Mountains of California have their own homegrown tall tale that, according to a long line of witnesses, is closer to fact than fiction. For those who have found themselves in the company of the dark things that haunt the range; the fear is real.

The Native American Chumash tribe were the first people known to have encountered the mysterious clan who are said to inhabit the mountains. To ensure that their experiences were not lost with the passage of time, they recorded them as a warning to future generations.

The entities that natives referred to as "The Old Ones," stood anywhere from seven to fifteen feet in height, each one walking with the aid of a hand-carved staff. They wore long cloaks as well as wide-brimmed hats that effectively hid their bodies and faces. Able to maneuver around the treacherous terrain with ease, it was clear to all who saw them that these towering figures were a lifeform that was something other than human.

Their formidable presence became a part of everyday life for the Chumash people, even though the two groups did not interact in anyway. Theirs was an alliance that depended on keeping a respectable distance from one another.

The presence of the otherworldly silhouettes was also noted by Spanish settlers who happened upon the area in the 1800s. They, too, had a name for the dark shapes that roamed the mountaintops: "Los Vigilantes Oscuros."

Not long after their arrival, the settlers realized that something unnatural owned the land after the sun went down. Night after night, groups of shadow figures could be seen standing in silent observance of all who passed by. They never moved nor did they utter a sound. Their job, as they saw it, was to keep a close watch on those who infringed on their territory.

Sightings of the "Dark Watchers," as they were later known, died down over the years only to resurface in the 1960s. New life was breathed into the legend when members of a hiking party, out for a nature walk, realized that they had company.

Among the hikers that afternoon was a high school principal who had decided to break from the group to do a bit of exploring on his own. Shortly after leaving the beaten path, he got the feeling that he was not alone. Looking up from the trail, he noticed a tall man, clad in dark attire, standing atop a large rock.

Taken aback by the sudden appearance of the stranger, the man immediately summoned his companions. They joined him within a matter of moments, but by then the dark figure had disappeared without a trace. This would be the first of many sightings that would occur in the coming years.

In 2013, Elizabeth Benitez of San Meteo, California claimed to have had her own run-in with a Dark Watcher. She and a friend were driving near the San Luis Obispo reservoir when she spotted an odd form standing at the foot of the mountains that abutted the highway.

A passenger in the car, Elizabeth described what she witnessed as having been an exceedingly tall individual, clothed entirely in black. She likened its appearance to that of the "Grim Reaper."

The woman could clearly see, even at some distance, that the thing standing near the road was not human. Elizabeth excitedly pointed out the remarkable sight to her friend who was driving. Looking away for a moment, the other woman witnessed the dark form leaning down over what appeared to be a large puddle of water.

As they passed by the imposing creature, Elizabeth begged her friend to find a place to turn around so they could get a second look. The driver, tired and not wanting to tempt fate, ignored the pleas and kept driving.

Also in 2013, a carful of people from Hollister, California insisted that they, too, encountered an unidentifiable figure while driving past the range. Having traveled the exact same route countless times in his life, the driver was surprised to see any sign of life in the remote area. As he got closer, he knew that the hunchbacked figure standing before them was like nothing he had ever seen before.

Clad in a long, dark cape and standing well over ten feet tall, the odd form resembled a bird of prey, but was much too large to have actually been one. Most worrisome to the man and his passengers was the fact that the creature showed no fear of the car or its occupants.

Shocked by what they had seen, the group circled around and returned to the same area, but found that the curious being had fled. The man returned to the same spot numerous times in the coming years, but never saw the cryptid again.

In 2015, a runner in training for an upcoming event happened to pass by the range one afternoon. As he darted past, he noticed a shadowy figure standing high above him in an area that no one would have been able to navigate without the aid of special safety equipment.

The man stood in stunned silence for a few seconds before going on his way. Realizing that he had witnessed something he probably shouldn't have, he tried to put the incident out of his mind. In time, he would convince himself that it had never happened at all.

Almost exactly one year to the day after the encounter, the marathoner went running in the same area and saw the figure again. No longer able to deny what he had clearly seen, not once, but twice; he decided it was best to find someplace else to train.

A hiker from Ojai kept company with an unknown being in 2018. While walking in a desolate spot near the foot of the mountains, he was suddenly conscious that someone was standing close by. Not wanting to seem impolite, the hiker waved to the other party who returned the gesture in same.

It was around that time that the man decided to take a break from his trek. Under the observant eye of the other fellow, he lit a cigarette and took a drag before slowly exhaling the smoke. This is where things took a bizarre turn that convinced the hiker that his accidental companion was not what he seemed.

As the bemused hiker watched, the dark figure mimicked the action he had just seen, blowing out a large puff of smoke into the air. This wouldn't have been a concern had it not been for the fact that he did not possess a cigarette or any other smoking implement.

Instantly aware that he was being studied by something completely foreign to him, the hiker took off running for his car. As he drove away, he could see that the dark visitor, apparently satisfied with the results of its experiment, was scaling the cliffs as easily as most people walk on solid ground.

The son of famed author John Steinbeck became infatuated with the Dark Watchers after having his own unexplained encounter with the legendary mountain dwellers. After his first sighting of the unearthly beings, he was inspired to pen a book dedicated to exploring their history. It seemed that anyone who found themselves in close proximity of these enigmas could never quite get past the experience.

Mountains have a mystique all their own. Reaching high into the sky, in the past, they have purportedly been home to gods, aliens and everything in between. The energy they possess attracts visitors from every realm imaginable and always has. That is, if one believes in such things.

There are those who are adamant that travelers from other galaxies used mountain peaks as meeting places with ancient man. They insist that extraterrestrials acted as guides and mentors to these primitives. The beginnings of civilization as we know it are thought to have taken shape under their tutelage.

Perhaps the Dark Watchers are living remnants of those times who not only survived, but thrived in areas virtually impenetrable by man. It is also possible that they are simply a group of society's castoffs who, beginning centuries ago, decided to isolate themselves from humanity.

The latter theory doesn't explain the multitude of eyewitness descriptions of extremely tall beings, carrying canes and adopting the posture of predatory birds. Nor does it answer the question of how they have managed to get by for so long without ever needing to visit populated areas for groceries, clothing or other provisions. Had such an event ever occurred, someone surely would have noticed a ten-foot tall birdman shopping at the five and dime.

The idea has been batted about that these figures are simply products of overactive imaginations. Navigating the long stretches of roadway that run along the foothills can be exhausting for even the most seasoned of travelers. After extended periods spent staring straight ahead at the seemingly endless asphalt, it has been suggested that the mind begins to play tricks on weary drivers.

If this scenario holds true, then the dark entities may very well be indigenous birds that seem much larger than they actually are to those passing through. This may be the event in some cases, but certainly not all.

Hikers out for a leisurely nature walk surely wouldn't be under the same duress as someone who has been sitting behind a steering wheel so long that they have lost all sense of reality. On the contrary, these visitors to the mountains should be in a heightened state of awareness. As such, their accounts of encounters with the Dark Watchers are difficult to write off as anxiety-induced hallucinations.

The legend of the living shadows of the Santa Lucia's continues today, just as it has for hundreds of years. Real or imagined, these entities have become synonymous with the mountain range. Those whose curiosity surpasses their common sense can check the region out for themselves as long as they remember to respect the locals. After all, in that particular neck of the woods, outlanders often find themselves in the minority.

Chapter 27:
The Licker

Most of us grow up following a bedtime ritual to which we must strictly adhere, lest we face dire consequences. This is, of course, making sure that our arms and legs are tucked under the covers before we drift off to the world of dreams. To forgo this most important act of self-preservation is to risk being grabbed by the monster that undoubtedly resides beneath our bed.

The fear of an unknown evil lurking in our rooms that bides its time until sleep takes over, rendering us powerless, is so universal that it has generated more than one urban legend. The most well-known of these spooky tales reminds all who hear it that, sometimes, the boogeyman is real and closer than we dare think.

The story begins with a news bulletin that flashes across the television screen. It warns residents of a small community to be on the lookout for a deranged killer who has escaped from a local asylum for the criminally insane.

Unfortunately for the teenaged girl whose favorite program has just been interrupted, her parents have gone out for the evening, leaving her home alone with only the family's collie to keep her company.

The girl listens intently as the newscaster implores viewers to lock all of their doors and windows. As soon as the station returns to the regularly scheduled program, the girl jumps up and does exactly as she was instructed.

After checking and double-checking every possible entrance into the house, the girl breathes a sigh of relief. Satisfied that everything is secure, she snuggles up with her dog and resumes watching the show.

It is after midnight when the girl decides that it's time to turn-in. Her parents are not yet home, but she knows that they won't be out much longer. As a precaution, she lets the dog, who usually sleeps in the basement, stay in her room for the rest of the night.

All is quiet as the girl and her faithful companion both fall asleep. At some point during the night, she rolls over onto her stomach, allowing her hand to dangle just above the floor. She is awakened shortly afterwards by the sensation of something warm and moist being dragged across both her palm and the back of her hand in turn.

Still half-asleep, the girl pulls the appendage away from what she assumes is the voracious licking of her dog. Now resting on her side, both hands folded under her face, the girl attempts to go back to sleep. The only thing preventing her from getting the much-needed shut-eye is a dripping sound coming from the adjoining bathroom.

The girl is annoyed with herself for having left the tap on, but her bed is so comfortable that she just can't bring herself to get up and walk across the cold floor to turn the nuisance off. As aggravating as it is, she decides that the leaky faucet can wait till morning. With that, she nods off for the remainder of the night.

Early the next morning, the girl gets up and stumbles into the bathroom, ill-prepared for what awaits her once she enters the tiny room. Noticing immediately that the floor is awash in a sticky liquid, the bewildered girl flips on the light switch. As her eyes focus in the blinding light, she lets out a scream that is loud enough to wake the neighbors.

What she sees will leave mental scars that cannot be healed. Hanging upside down from the shower rod is the body of the family dog. The beloved pet, now barely recognizable, has been skinned clean to the bone.

The girl's parents rush to their daughter's room as soon as they hear her piercing screams. As they lead the distraught teenager away from the grisly scene in the lavatory, they notice writing on the bedroom wall.

The message, presumably left by whoever killed the dog, is as simple as it is savage. It reads, "Humans can lick, too."

It is later determined by investigators that the escaped lunatic had entered the house by way of an unlocked window hours before the "BOTL" had been broadcast. Little did the girl know, but the killer had been right under her nose all along.

In a variation of the tale, the parents come home and check on their daughter. Finding her sleeping peacefully, they escort the dog out of her room and into the basement. While downstairs, the father notices an open window. When he attempts to close it, he discovers that the lock is broken.

Well-aware that an escaped killer is on the loose, he does the best he can to secure the window before joining his wife upstairs. The two of them discuss the matter of the broken latch for a short time before deciding that it is silly to worry about such a minor detail. After all, what were the odds that a maniac would target their house when there were so many others to choose from?

The rest of the story remains the same, ending with the discovery of the mutilated dog and the warning printed in its blood.

The aforementioned incident allegedly took place in the 1960s in the Midwestern United States. The exact location varies depending upon the source, but it is thought to have been either Farmersburg, Indiana or a town in Iowa by the same name. No official records exist of the events ever having occurred, but that didn't stop the tale from taking on a life of its own.

It is widely accepted that this particular story is more fiction than fact. Most likely created as a cautionary tale for teenagers getting their first taste of freedom; the harrowing story acts as a reminder to those on the cusp of adulthood that the real world is chock full of hidden dangers.

Writer D.B. Martin penned a short story in 1982 titled *Bedtime for Sam* that closely mirrors this gruesome tale. Although the events that spawned the urban legend were said to have occurred in the 1960s, he is often credited with planting the original seed.

Scary near-misses involving intruders are not limited to teenagers left on their own. In another case of "believe it or don't" a woman returns home, exhausted, from a long day's work. Forgoing a meal or shower, she heads straight for bed. Just as she enters her room, she catches a glimpse of someone sliding underneath the bed.

Thinking fast, she loudly exclaims that she forgot to lock up her bike for the night. She quickly exits the apartment, all the while berating herself for being so thoughtless. Once she is in the clear, she runs to a neighbor's home where she phones the police.

Arriving minutes later, officers find the man secreted away under the woman's bed. Beside him on the floor, gleaming in the beam of their flashlights, lay a butcher knife. As he is led away in handcuffs, the man calmly explains that he only wanted to see what she looked like on the inside.

It wasn't lost on the woman that, had she stopped to make a sandwich or take a hot bath, she wouldn't have seen the man as he retreated to his hiding place. Likewise, if she had entered the bedroom a split second later, she would have been at his mercy.

The suspect was deemed mentally unfit to stand trial. Unable to comprehend the reasons for his actions, the man was committed to a long-term psychiatric facility where, as far as anyone knows, he remains to this day.

In 2005, a somewhat similar incident occurred when a man took his obsession with a coworker to frightening extremes. The entire ordeal began with a chance meeting on the grounds of Holy Cross Hospital in Silver Spring, Maryland.

Michelle Fredenburg-Onion was already in a committed relationship when the hospital valet set his sights on her. As far as she was concerned, Carlos Castellanos-Feria was the friendly guy who parked her car and nothing more.

The two had spoken briefly on only a handful of occasions, but that had been enough for Carlos. Smitten with her warmth and beauty, Michelle became the object of his desire. In no time at all, he had formulated a plan that would put him front and center in her life, whether she wanted him there or not.

The whole thing started innocently enough one morning when Michelle, who worked in the physical therapy department, handed her keys over to Carlos in his capacity as valet. It was something she had done numerous times in the past with no worries. She had no reason to think that this occasion would be any different.

Michelle didn't know it at the time, but she had given Carlos just the thing he needed to gain unlimited access to her life, namely, her keychain. Later that day, while on break, he had copies made of her keys, including the one to her apartment. At the end of her shift, Michelle's car was delivered to her and she headed home, unaware that her trust had been breached.

Carlos had observed Michelle's comings and goings until he knew her schedule like the back of his hand. Taking full advantage of that ill-gotten knowledge, he used his key to enter her apartment as soon as the opportunity presented itself. Once inside, he wasted no time getting down to business.

In the coming days, Michelle's stalker set up cameras in the bedroom so that he could film any activity that happened to occur there. He also made a place for himself under the bed. Among other things, he stocked the area with toiletries, snacks and a change of clothes. All that was left to do was to lie in the dark and wait for Michelle to come home.

Two days would pass before Michelle's boyfriend discovered the stalker's nest underneath the bed. After finding notebooks detailing his girlfriend's activities, explicit videotapes, cameras and a power cord in the relatively small space, he phoned police. The couple was thoroughly shaken by the blatant invasion of privacy. As it turned out, they didn't know the half of it.

With so much evidence at their disposal, it wasn't long before authorities zeroed in on a likely suspect. Carlos was arrested and brought in for questioning. He admitted his wrongdoing, up to a point. Although he swore that his motives were pure, unused condoms and latex gloves had also been discovered in his hideaway leading investigators to believe that the mild-mannered valet wasn't as harmless as he was letting on.

In 2006, Carlos Castellanos-Feria was tried and convicted on charges of stalking and burglary. He received a three-year sentence which means that he is a free man today. Michelle, on the other hand, says that she lives her life on pins and needles, never fully able to feel comfortable in her surroundings. For her, the monster under the bed was terrifyingly real.

Chapter 28:
The Swamp Grunch

Tales of cryptids can be found far and wide. In most instances, the alleged sightings of these unidentified beings are so absurd that no one takes them seriously. However, on rare occasions, a story comes along that is so gripping it gives birth to an urban legend. Such is the case with the Louisiana Grunch.

This bit of lore was born in the bayou in the 1700s when settlers claimed to have encountered something in the deep woods that was nothing short of the devil's spawn. The atrocity was said to have sported the head of a goat and a body that was a cross between an ape and a large reptile. With a mouth full of razor-sharp teeth and the claws of a tiger, the swamp beast could cut through its prey like a hot knife through butter.

According to legend, the nasty creature had two tells that announced its presence. The first was a high-pitched whistle that was just this side of a banshee's shriek. The second was the overpowering stench of something long-dead and rotting which would fill the air as the source of the squealing closed in on its target. The end result was not pleasant for those dim-witted enough to miss these cues.

Stories of the otherworldly beings that lived in the murk and subsisted on the blood of mammals continued to make the rounds for centuries. Much like vampires and werewolves, it was believed that anyone who survived a bite from one of these creatures would be cursed to join their ranks. This tactic ensured their survival as a species, as the populace of New Orleans and the surrounding areas would come to know all too well.

In the 1950s, a new breed of these opportunistic feeders surfaced. Bolder than their ancestors, who preferred the isolation of the backwoods, these upstarts stalked the roadways in search of fresh blood meals.

The first reported sightings occurred near the community of Little Woods. It was there that folks who either took a wrong turn or simply pulled off the main road to take a quick nap would find themselves on an old dirt pathway that dead-ended deep in the marsh. It was only when they heard the shrill screams emanating from somewhere beneath the cypress trees that they realized they might be in trouble.

With nowhere to turn around, the panicked drivers would be in a tizzy as they tried to figure a way out of their predicament. The situation was made all the worse by the knowledge that the ear-splitting shrieks were growing closer by the second. They couldn't help but wonder what sort of animal was responsible for the ungodly cries. The answer would come soon enough.

As they watched in disbelief, a creature would slowly emerge from the woods. Those who escaped to tell the tale described it as being an offence to the senses in every way. Standing about four feet tall, the source of the squawking was a half-goat, half-primate albino with abnormally large eyes that glowed red in the darkness.

Before the motorist could react, the freakish being would pounce on the vehicle and begin ripping away at the steel doors in an attempt to gain access to the feast that was just out of reach. Even with the windows rolled up and the vents closed, the air would be filled with the putrid odor of decay.

Knowing that they were only inches away from a grisly death, the driver's survival instincts would usually kick in around this time. Putting the car in reverse and hitting the gas, they would barrel out of the bog. As dangerous an action as it was, they knew that driving backwards at full speed was still a safer bet than facing whatever the swamp monster had in store.

For over thirty years, missing persons' reports were said to have piled up on the local sheriff's desk. Many of those were fishermen who would set out in the morning for a leisurely day spent casting their lines into their favorite watering holes. Hours later, when they didn't return home, their families would go searching for them. On some occasions, their gear would be found along with a cache of freshly caught fish. Everything was accounted for except for the fishermen who were never seen or heard from again.

As more and more people came forward with stories of encounters with the swamp creatures, area residents made the connection between the missing men and the mutants said to inhabit the swamplands. Since most of the sightings had taken place in the vicinity of Grunch Road, the beasts assumed to be responsible for the rash of disappearances became known as "Grunch."

There are some who believe that the Grunch where sent from hell originally to act as protectors of the devil's minions on earth. Somewhere along the line, these agents lost sight of their duties. Rather that fulfilling their purpose, they used their powers to prey on any warm-blooded creature that happened to cross their path.

Banished from Hades for their insolence, these demonic forces eventually settled in the Louisiana bogs. As punishment for defying the hierarchy of the netherworld, they were condemned to spend an eternity tormented by an unquenchable thirst for blood. Forced into a never-ending quest for sustenance, the hunt they once enjoyed soon became the bane of their existence.

Others theorize that the Grunch were the product of inbreeding. They claim that it all started back in the early 1900s when a band of outcasts packed up their belongings and set up their own society in the recesses of the swamp.

The group, which consisted mostly of dwarves and albinos, had spent their lives being made to feel like they didn't belong. Ridiculed and abused from early childhood, they had finally had enough. It would be in the heart of the swamp that they would at last find solace.

Although many members of this newly established community were related, it didn't stop them from reproducing. Some of their offspring were born with no obvious defects. Others, however, were considered barely human, even by their own parents. It was these unfortunate souls who would later be labeled "swamp monsters."

Reviled and feared by those who brought them into the world; these mutants were sent out into the woods to survive on their own as soon as they were old enough. Teaching themselves to hunt, they thrived in their new environment. They learned quickly that blood nourished them and kept them strong.

When their food supply dwindled, the Grunch devised an ingenious way to snare unsuspecting prey. One of their favorite methods was to place an injured animal, usually a goat, in the middle of the road that led into the swamp. They would then hunker down in the brush and wait for their bait to draw the attention of a sympathetic human.

If things went off without a hitch, a car would stop as soon as the driver caught sight of the animal in distress. As the Good Samaritan rushed to render aid, the Grunch would descend upon them from their hiding places. A feeding frenzy would then ensue. Afterwards, the vehicle would be pushed into the swamp where it would eventually be swallowed up by the vegetation.

Having lived in the wetlands their whole lives, the Grunch could navigate the murky water and thick mud with ease. Not so their quarry. Sometimes, just for sport, rather than killing their victims on the spot, they would throw them in quicksand and watch with amusement as they struggled to free themselves. Just as the muck was about to swallow them whole, the flailing prey would be pulled to the surface by their captors. The reprieve would be short-lived as the Grunch would then serve them a fate far worse than the one they had narrowly escaped.

As unholy a presence as they may have been, these swamp dwellers never forgot where they came from. The only humans who were safe around them were the ones who put them in their predicament in the first place. Although they had shown them little mercy, the parents and siblings of those deemed unworthy to live among the outcasts were revered by the obscenities they themselves had created.

Before long, the Grunch began to reproduce which perpetuated this unconventional species. Each generation was stronger than the last. In time, this new breed lost all resemblance to the humans they once were. It is these descendants who are alleged to reside in the swamp today.

Parts of the legend of the Grunch have their basis in actual events. Beginning in the 1950s, a group of New Orleans residents decided that city life just wasn't for them. Preferring the idea of living off the grid, they moved trailers into the woods where they then set up house.

These swamp people were some of the first in modern times to speak of the strange creatures with which they shared the marshlands. They knew going in that they would be living amongst alligators and snakes; they didn't realize at the time that these creepy-crawlers were only the tip of the iceberg.

The residents of the swamps claimed that they heard whistling and shrieking sounds during the night that didn't belong to any form of wildlife that they knew of. Those who happened to catch a glimpse of the source of the noise never forgot the sight.

The creatures emitting the screeches stood less than five feet tall. They were said to walk just as well on two legs as four. Sporting long hair all over their bodies, cloven hooves and talons on their fingers, they were terrifying to behold.

The animal, if that was what it was, supposedly existed in a state of constant agitation. It was believed that it would attack not only when threatened or hungry, but also for pleasure. No one who saw one from a distance wanted any part of meeting this anomaly of nature up close.

Sightings died down in the 1980s when plans got underway to develop the area. The trailers and their occupants were removed in preparation for the land to be razed. Since a new byway was also in the works, Grunch Road was rendered obsolete. Over time, it would disappear in the overgrowth.

All was quiet until 2005 when Hurricane Katrina dealt a devastating blow to the state. Beginning shortly thereafter, reports of run-ins with unidentified swamp creatures skyrocketed. The Grunch, for all intents and purposes, had made a comeback.

One of the earliest reports came from a woman who claimed to have had an odd encounter while driving around surveying storm damage. It was just after dark when she happened to catch sight of a figure like nothing she had ever seen before.

She described the thing she saw skulking along at the side of the road that night as having the combined characteristics of a monkey, lizard and dog. Rather than being covered in fur, it was scaly in appearance. She added that it had the long snout of an alligator, but the nostrils and facial features of an ape.

The creature walked upright on two legs, standing somewhere between four and five feet in height. When it realized that it had been seen, the woman said that it let out a sound that was akin to a screaming hiss.

As she drove past the beastly form, it made a half-hearted attempt to reach for the woman's car. She would later say that the strange life form had been too lackluster to have posed any real threat. All the same, she didn't want to take the chance that it would get its second wind. She sped from the scene as quickly as possible.

Dozens of sightings were cataloged in the years following Katrina. It was a widely held notion that what many witnesses were claiming to be monsters were, in actuality, run-of-the-mill swamp denizens that had been displaced by the ravages of the hurricane.

No eyewitness accounts of encounters with anything resembling a Grunch have been documented in over a decade. Of course, this doesn't mean that none have occurred. If the past is any indicator, it is a safe bet that these creatures, real or imagined, will experience a rebirth. That is, assuming, that they haven't already done so.

Chapter 29:
The Alice Killings

Accounts of crazed killers on the loose certainly have a monopoly when it comes to urban myths. One of the most famous of these was said to have occurred in Japan in the span between 1999 and 2005. Dubbed "The Alice Killings," they would leave people wondering, to this day, where to separate fact from fiction.

The nightmare began with the brutal murder of a restaurant worker named Sasaki Megumi. On what would turn out to be the last night of her life, the twenty-nine year old cook spent the evening partying with friends. Tiring of the festivities, she left alone, on foot, sometime after midnight.

No one knows for sure what happened after that except, of course, for her killer. Later on that morning, Megumi's body was discovered by a couple out for a leisurely walk. The pair knew something was wrong when they spotted streaks of blood that led into a tree-lined area of a nearby park.

Worried that someone might be in trouble, they followed the trail until they came upon a ghastly sight. Hanging from the branches of the flowering trees, were the dismembered limbs of Sasaki Megumi. Her torso and head were lying in the grass along with her personal possessions.

Police were immediately informed and a murder investigation was launched. The killer, or killers, had left them little to go on. One clue that was found at the scene would pique the interest of both investigators and the public.

Alongside the victim's purse and clothing, a single playing card had been deliberately placed in a spot where it could not be missed. Authorities were instantly aware that the item had not belonged to Megumi. Scrawled across the front of the card, presumably in the victim's blood, was the word "Alice."

Nearly two years would pass without a break in the case. Then, in February of 2001, the killer struck again. The second victim was the singer in a popular local band. Yamene Akio had played what would turn out to be his final show at a local bar on the night he went missing.

Following the performance, closed-circuit cameras captured images of Akio as he returned to his apartment. A few minutes later, footage showed a figure, clad in a long black cloak, entering the building through a side door. He is then seen walking down the corridor that led to Akio's flat.

Several minutes tick by before the man reenters the frame. This time, he is dragging a large trash bag behind him. Even in the grainy video, it is clear that something is struggling inside the sack. The man keeps his head down as he passes the surveillance cameras, making identification impossible.

Exactly one week to the day after the singer's disappearance, a bar owner was greeted by a macabre sight when he arrived at his establishment. There, propped up at one of the tables, sat the body of Yamene Akio. In his hand, he held a playing card; the king of diamonds. Written in blood, just as in the previous instance, was the name "Alice."

An autopsy showed that the cause of death had been a single gunshot wound to the head. The victim had also suffered a gaping wound to his throat by which his vocal cords had been ripped out. Ironically, Akio's final show had taken place at the very bar in which his body was discovered.

Investigators knew that the playing card was a clue that had been intentionally left behind by the killer. What they couldn't sort out was how the mysterious "Alice" figured into the equation. With two murders under his belt, police wondered when and where the psychopath would strike next. They wouldn't have to wait long to find out.

Kai Sakura was a teenager without an enemy in the world when her life was arbitrarily cut short. Abducted on her way home from school, her remains turned up two days after she was reported missing by her distraught parents.

She was found buried in a shallow grave embellished with a card depicting the queen of clubs and bearing the signature "Alice." Sakura's body had been brutalized in ways that sickened even the most hardened detectives.

The teen had been skinned, probably while still alive. Both of her eyes had been extracted, a subliminal sign that she had perhaps known her killer. As a finishing touch, a crown had been meticulously sewn onto her scalp.

This murder stood apart from the others, not only for the severity of the mutilation, but also because the killer attached a letter to the corpse. The note read, "Death is a distorted dream. It will always rule. The one who died is lucky."

The bizarre collection of nonsense phrases did nothing to further the investigation. If anything, it only convinced detectives of what they already suspected, namely, that they were dealing with a madman. Worse still, they knew beyond a shadow of doubt that he was only getting started.

The fourth and fifth victims were Hina Oshiro and her brother Hayato. The youngsters' bodies were discovered in their beds by their parents on April 4, 2005. It was later determined that both children had been injected with a poisonous mixture of chemicals.

Each of the siblings clutched half of the ace of hearts in their tiny hands; when the pieces were placed together, the letters spelled out the now familiar "Alice." Detectives scrambled to find a connection between this new clue and the victims. Their efforts would lead to another dead end.

Investigators caught a break shortly after the murders of the brother and sister when a vagrant was picked up after he was seen wearing a trench coat that had belonged to Yamene Akio. The case shifted into overdrive when traces of dried blood were detected on the garment.

Suzuko Yuuto had a long history of mental health issues. Homeless at the time of his arrest, he was known locally as a harmless oddball. When questioned in regards to the killings, he claimed that he had no knowledge of the crimes or the victims.

According to Yuuto, the coat had been gifted to him by a "demon man" he met on the streets. He described his benefactor as having been dressed head-to-toe in a black shroud. The figure had not spoken a word to him. The stranger had simply handed him the coat and walked away. Yuuto added, as an aside, that he had been close enough to the man to see that he had no face.

It wasn't lost on the agents in charge of the case that the dark figure Yuuto described matched the suspect seen on the surveillance cameras in Akio's building. As unbelievable as his story sounded, that one element rang true.

Witnesses soon came forward to attest to Yuuto's innocence. Luckily for the prime suspect, he had been seen by dozens of people at a homeless shelter over five miles from Akio's apartment on the night he went missing.

Since Yuuto could not possibly have been at both locations at the same time, the case against him fell apart. Citing a lack of evidence, officials released Yuuto from custody without any charges being filed. Fading into the world of the homeless and forgotten, he returned to a life of obscurity.

The murders of the Oshiro siblings were the last ones attributed to the fiend who signed his work with a playing card. No similar cases have been reported in the intervening years. The case remains unsolved, although detectives who were involved in the initial investigation have never given up their quest to find the killer.

It has been speculated that the story that morphed into The Alice Killings had its beginnings in a song by a Japanese artist known as Yugami-P. Titled "Hitobashira Arisu" or "Human Sacrifice Alice," it basically outlines the events depicted in the urban legend. Others dismiss this as a coincidence and nothing more.

That being said, there are still scores of netizens who assert that The Alice Killings are based on true events. The murders supposedly occurred in the city of Sapporo in the early 2000s. The circumstances of those crimes, if they did indeed occur, closely match the ones depicted in the urban legend.

The names of the victims are said to have been changed, along with a few other minor details, but the acts depicted are the same. So, regrettably, is the outcome. In the actual case, just as in the urban legend, the killings stopped as quickly as they began. Similarly, investigators filed the case away as "unsolved," at least for the time being.

The existence of a lunatic who deposited playing cards at crime scenes in Japan may be in question, but it is undisputed that such a specimen did stalk the streets of Spain during roughly the same timeframe. His name is Alfredo Galan (Sotillo), better known in his home country as "The Playing Card Killer."

Galan was a former military officer who, for reasons even he couldn't explain, snapped in the early months of 2003. What followed was a killing spree that would leave six victims, all strangers to their assailant, dead and two others seriously injured.

The killer's preferred method of execution was a gunshot fired at point-blank range, usually from behind. Some of his crimes were committed in broad daylight in full view of witnesses. His first known victim was shot while playing in a public park with his two-year old son. The traumatized child was by his father's side when the fatal blow was struck.

After the murder, a playing card had fallen from Galan's coat pocket. The shooter, who had been in a hurry to leave, was unaware that he had left anything behind. It was only after he saw news reports of the strange find that he realized his blunder. After giving it some thought, he decided to incorporate the gesture into his crimes.

The remorseless killer would go on to claim five more lives over the next few weeks. At each location, he would leave a playing card near the body of his victim.

Galan's murderous rampage would, thankfully, be short-lived. He was apprehended in July of 2003, bringing the ugly chapter to a close. Tried and convicted of the six slayings, Galan received a one hundred forty-two year prison sentence.

The story of The Alice Killings has been fodder for horror enthusiasts for well over a decade. It has been the subject of both television anthology series' and feature films. The fascination with an unidentified individual who kills without rhyme or reason is one that is quick to capture our imaginations. Adding playing cards, symbolic in their own right, to the mix only serves to sweeten the pot. In the end, real or fantasy, it's a tale worth telling.

Chapter 30:
The Death Car

Superstition tells us that to purchase an object that has a stigma attached is to tempt fate. A car that has been involved in a previous accident, for instance, is one that was meant to be destroyed, but somehow persisted. Such an occurrence might be a stroke of luck for the vehicle, but it does not bode well for owners yet to come.

Death cars, as they are known, also have a place in this collection of urban legends. As this one goes, a fellow leafing through a local newspaper happens to spy an advertisement that grabs his attention.

In the "Used Car" section, someone has posted a luxury sedan for sale. The man does a double take when he sees the asking price. Although certainly not an expert, he knows that the amount is only a fraction of what such a high-end vehicle is worth.

Intrigued, the potential buyer phones the number attached to the listing and speaks to someone he presumes to be the owner. They exchange small talk for a few minutes before the seller throws out a bit of information that sheds light on why he is practically giving the car away.

Getting right to the point, the owner explains that his brother killed himself inside the vehicle by running a hose from the exhaust pipe into the interior. Since he lived alone, the man's body had not been found for over a week.

As one can imagine, the smell of decomposition hung heavily in the air when the remains were discovered. According to the surviving brother, no amount of cleaning or disinfecting could get rid of the stench of death.

The man who is making the inquiry remains silent as he processes the disturbing information he has just been given. A practical thinker by nature, he decides that, with proper detailing, the odor could be neutralized. He figures that, once the car is in tip-top shape, he can resell it and reap the rewards of his investment.

A sly businessman, the buyer manages to convince the owner to bring the already low price down to an embarrassingly paltry sum before sealing the deal. When all is said and done, he meets up with the seller and hands over the cash in exchange for the vehicle. Even as the deal is being brokered, the smell of something long-dead pollutes the air around the otherwise pristine car.

Plans seldom work out the way they are intended and this time was no exception. The buyer's ordeal begins as soon as he drops the car off at a restoration shop to have it thoroughly cleaned. The workers, upon inspecting the interior, refuse to do the job. One of the men, in fact, is taken ill as soon as he opens the door.

The buyer, too, begins to experience a throbbing pain in his temple anytime he sits behind the wheel of his newly purchased automobile. He is also stricken with a tightness in his chest that only subsides when he is clear of the sedan.

The final straw comes one day when the man is attempting to clean the interior of the car. While scrubbing the seats with soap, he suddenly finds himself gasping for air. Unable to catch his breath, he tumbles out of the open driver's side door and onto the pavement.

As soon as he hits the ground, his breathing returns to normal. The man wants to believe that his episode is simply a reaction to the chemicals, but he knows that something else is going on. Even though there is no logical explanation for it, he feels that the problem isn't the cleaning agents, but the car itself.

Thoroughly convinced that if he keeps the car he will suffer the same fate as the original owner, the man opts to pawn it off on someone else. Asking for the same amount that he had paid, he quickly unloads the vehicle he now believes carries a death curse.

Before long, the next owner experiences a series of unexplained medical emergencies. As it turns out, the smell is the least of the car's problems. More worrisome for the succession of people unfortunate to purchase the sedan is the sensation of having their life's breath stolen anytime they get behind the wheel.

As the car passes from one owner to another, someone finally makes the connection between the original owner's death by carbon monoxide poisoning and the feeling of being strangled that everyone who finds themselves in possession of the vehicle experiences.

The story usually ends with the car being hauled away as scrap or by it simply disappearing with no one knowing where it ends up. The latter, of course, gives rise to the fear that this most sinister of cars is still out there somewhere, claiming victims anytime the opportunity arises.

The real story of the death car is believed to have occurred in 1938 In Mecosta, Michigan. It was there that a man, known only as "Mr. Demings," committed suicide inside of his cherished Model-A Ford in the aftermath of a bitter break-up with his girlfriend.

It was on a hot August evening that Demings ended his life on the side of a desolate back road. No one knew at the time what had become of him. Close family and friends acknowledged that he was upset, but they had not known the depths of his despair until it was too late.

In October, hunters happened upon the car that contained the remains of young Mr. Demings. As one can imagine, two months spent baking in the sun had not been kind to the remains. Much like in the urban legend, nothing known to man could purge the car of the noxious smell of decay that had attached itself to the interior.

No one reported being choked within an inch of their life while behind the wheel of the ill-fated vehicle, but it was deemed unsalvageable nonetheless. When extensive cleaning, not to mention reupholstering, failed to banish the odor, the car was dismantled and sold for parts. This story illustrates that once something has been marked by the hand of death, there is no going back to the way things once were.

Chapter 31:
The Ghosts of the Woods

The legend of the white deer is one that has been around for centuries. These albinos are viewed by many, not as genetic mutations, but as supernatural beings. To kill one of these mystical creatures all but ensures that the offender will meet their maker sooner than later.

The theory behind this urban legend stems from the belief that white deer are representatives of the spirit world. Known as "The Ghosts of the Woods," these magnificent beings are thought to house reincarnated human souls. To purposely take one of these lives is considered an unforgivable sin. In order to make things right, another life must be offered as an act of atonement for the egregious misdeed.

One often repeated story involving a white deer tells of a group of teenagers who congregate for a morning of deer hunting. Upon their arrival in the woods, they branch off in different directions, agreeing to meet up in a couple of hours.

When the time comes to regroup, they all gather at the rendezvous point. All, that is, except for one. Assuming that the absentee has gotten lost in the hunt, a search ensues. He is found, deep in the woods, writhing on the ground in the throes of a violent seizure.

The boy's panicked friends attempt to render aid, but nothing they do seems to help. Knowing that his life may hang in the balance, they hurriedly carry him to the clearing where their vehicles are parked. From there, they race to the nearest hospital, the boy still seizing in the backseat.

Even as they were tending to the stricken teen, they couldn't help but notice that, lying beside him in the grass had been the body of a white stag. Its eyes still glistening, the deer had obviously been killed a short time earlier. The occupants of the car were all thinking the same thing, but no one spoke of it out loud. Their friend, they feared, had unleashed a curse.

By the time the boy received treatment for the seizure, the damage had already been done. Although he survived, his life was forever changed. Unable to perform even the simplest tasks, he became dependent on others for his care.

The other members of the group admitted that they had been aware of the curse of the white deer for as long as they could remember. Many of them had been told about it by experienced woodsmen who believed that the legend was real.

After their friend had been stabilized at the hospital, a few of them had gone back to the woods to retrieve the body of the stag. When they reached the spot where its body had lain, there was nothing there, not even a single drop of blood.

The events of that day were especially troubling given that the boys had made a pact that they would not kill one of the rare creatures in the unlikely event that one should cross their path. They could never figure out what made their friend go back on his word.

For his part, the boy who killed the deer made no excuses for what he had done. He had simply acted on a whim only to learn the hard way that a decision made in haste can have repercussions that last a lifetime.

Another incident involved two men who were present when a white deer was harvested. One would die six months later from a massive heart attack. The other was killed in a car accident less than a year later near the exact spot where the hunt had taken place.

The Chickasaw tribe believes that the appearance of a white deer precipitates great change on the horizon. To take the life of the messenger is to change the path that was being prepared. Bad luck will follow as punishment for having thwarted the intentions of the spirits.

The stories of the white deer and that of the death car became intertwined in 1914 when a series of events would lay the groundwork for the onset of World War I. It all began on the streets of Sarajevo in what was then Hungary.

It was in June of 1914 that Austrian Archduke Franz Ferdinand and his wife Sophie were riding in a motorcade through the streets of the city, surrounded by throngs of supporters and well-wishers. The 1910 Graf & Stift Double Phaeton that carried them struck an imposing figure as it crawled in the bumper-to-bumper traffic.

Chaos erupted without warning when a grenade was thrown at the archduke's car from somewhere in the crowd. Miraculously, the explosive missed its target, bouncing off the roof and landing in the vehicle behind them.

The archduke and his wife were not injured, but the same could not be said for those riding in the car that was hit. Several members of the entourage were rushed to the hospital to be treated for their injuries, some of which were life-threatening.

Against the orders of his security detail, Ferdinand insisted on stopping by the hospital to pay his respects. This small act of kindness would change not only the timetable, but also the route of the motorcade. Without knowing it, the archduke had set in motion events that would shape generations to come.

Following their brief visit, Ferdinand and Sophie were once again making their way along the congested streets. The last-minute hospital detour had caused traffic to slow to a standstill. Sitting in the Double Phaeton with no way of moving forward or back, the couple were sitting ducks.

Seizing on this unexpected opportunity, a nineteen-year old Serbian nationalist named Gavrilo Princip made his move. As thousands of supporters waved and cheered, unaware of what was about to happen, shots rang out.

Princip, hedged in by the throngs, had fired wildly in the direction of the archduke's car. He managed to get off two shots before being overpowered by onlookers. Amazingly, both shots hit their marks.

Without taking aim, the assassin had hit Sophie in the stomach and her husband in the neck. Mortally wounded, both would die later that afternoon at the same hospital they had visited only hours prior to the shooting.

The car in which they were riding would go on to change hands no fewer than fifteen times in the coming years. One accident after another ensued, resulting in the deaths of thirteen people associated with the tainted automobile.

A theory was batted about that suggested that the car had held a lone soul that, after witnessing the killings of Ferdinand and Sophie, laid a curse upon all future owners. As preposterous as this notion may have been, no reasonable explanations could be found for the bad luck that befell those who subsequently came in contact with the doomed vehicle.

Oddly, the license plate on the car, which had not been altered, bore the numerical series III 118. Coincidentally, or maybe not, November 11, 1918 was the date in which WWI ended. Since the archduke's assassination had helped to trigger the war, many took this to mean that the events of that June day had been predicted long before they actually occurred.

Today, the Double Phaeton sits in the Museum of Military History in Vienna, Austria. Patrons are welcome to look, but not touch the possibly cursed limousine. No longer a threat to anyone or anything, it stands solely as a reminder that fate, once set in motion, has to run its course.

The story does not end there. It seems that Franz Ferdinand was an avid hunter; some might say that it was his life's obsession. After his death, it was discovered that he had kept meticulous records of his many kills. By his own count, he had been responsible for the deaths of over two-hundred thousand animals in his fifty years of life.

One of those kills had involved, of all things, a white deer. In 1913, the year before his assassination, the archduke had happened upon the rare creature while on a routine hunt. Without a moment's hesitation, he had taken its life.

Those closest to Ferdinand would later claim that he had been almost immediately stricken with regret. Fully aware of the curse associated with killing a white deer, the nagging fear that a life would have to be sacrificed in order to make things right weighed heavily on his conscience.

Ferdinand had bemoaned the premature death he felt sure was coming to all who would listen. He also worried that his wife or one of his children might be taken in his stead. The man who had never shown fear of anything in the past was now convinced that he was being stalked by the Grim Reaper.

It is possible that his strong belief in the curse had been at the root of his sudden lackadaisical approach to personal security. This might explain why he broke protocol and insisted on changing the course taken by the procession on the last day of his life. Or, as many believe, the events to come were destiny. There are those who still wonder if the circumstances that would eventually lead to WWI began, not on a battlefield, but on a hunting trip.

Chapter 32:
Zombie Road

Lawler Ford Road is a two-mile stretch that winds through the backcountry of Missouri. Located in the town of Wildwood, it is rumored to be a portal to, if not hell, then some other dark place where tormented souls constantly search for a means of escape. They would find it on what would come to be known as "Zombie Road."

The backstory of this notorious byway begins long before the pavement was laid. In the mid-1800s, a railroad was constructed along the Meramec River that ran from St. Louis all the way west. In the process of priming the land and laying the tracks, numerous workers lost their lives. After the trains started running, the number of deaths only increased.

News of someone or other being struck by a locomotive became commonplace. Although some of the victims were caught off guard as they crossed the railroad bridge, others who were on open land could have made it to safety but didn't.

No one could ever figure out why those attempting to maneuver the tracks hadn't moved to the side when they heard the trains approaching. Time and again, for reasons known only to the ones who perished on the rails, they had stubbornly insisted on participating in a challenge they were sure to lose.

A few years down the line, townspeople began to report strange lights that they had witnessed moving about in the surrounding woods. The same mysterious luminaries were also spotted along the roadsides. Along with the lights, shadows traveling independently in plain view of whoever happened to be passing by were also encountered in the vicinity of the train tracks.

Given the history of the area, it was difficult to pinpoint the source of the disturbances. Besides the deaths linked to the railroad, the waters of the Meramec had also claimed countless lives over the years.

The river has always been notoriously unpredictable. Calm one minute, raging the next, anyone setting out on the water was taking their life into their own hands. Many a homesteader never returned once they entered the mouth of the river.

Children were not immune to the voracious appetite of the Meramec. Drawn to the water's edge by curiosity, they would be summarily swept away as soon as they stepped foot past the shoreline.

Lawler Ford Road was a direct route, not only to the river, but also to the train tracks. As part of this haunted trio; it soon gained a nightmarish reputation that far surpassed the rest. It would be on this relatively short span that everything from demons to reanimated corpses were said to congregate.

It was sometime in the 1950s that the area received the unofficial title of "Zombie Road." According to lore, a patient had escaped from an insane asylum and somehow found his way to the road by following the trains.

No one knows for sure what became of him after he reached his destination. Upon searching the outlying area, authorities discovered a torn hospital gown that was soaked with blood. The find convinced them that the patient had probably been killed by a predator that had then dragged the body away to consume at its leisure.

Staff at the escapee's former institution had nicknamed the man "Zombie" due to his unresponsiveness and complete detachment from his fellow residents. Those in charge of his care had assumed that he was mentally unaware of his surroundings. That is, until the night of his escape.

Since the man's remains were never recovered, rumors swirled as to his fate. Some whispered that he had been hit by a train shortly after his daring run for freedom. In this scenario, the dazed man, unfamiliar with the area, had walked straight into the path of an oncoming locomotive. The force of the impact had torn the gown from his body as it carried him off to parts unknown.

Others believed that he had doffed the gown and left it behind to throw searchers off the trail. Foraging in the woods for food, he had learned to survive by killing and eating small game. Over the years, he supposedly moved on to bigger game. Adept at the hunt, he did not limit himself to four-legged prey.

Tales of a serial killer known as "The Zombie" soon made the rounds. Whether this monster was the escaped mental patient or an unidentified entity, no one could say. Regardless, everyone knew that to walk the road after dark was to risk coming face to face with something that, if it ever had been human, wasn't anymore.

It was also in the 1950s that the area gained a reputation as a crossroads. These points where worlds collide are thought to teem with otherworldly entities. This particular junction is reputedly a site where satanic rituals were performed that conjured up demons that should never have been permitted to walk this plane.

Dark, isolated and shrouded by trees, it was the perfect place to open doors that led to other dimensions. Once this was accomplished, spirits, both malevolent and benign, were called forth from beyond and invited to remain in this realm. It is these misplaced visitors who some believe are the true terrors of Zombie Road.

Another terrifying presence said to haunt Zombie Road is the ghost of Della Hamilton McCullough. The wife of a prominent judge, she was killed on the railway in 1876. Her spirit, unable to accept its sudden departure, is thought to remain bound to the tracks to this day. Often appearing as a hazy white apparition, she is a common sight for those who find themselves in the vicinity of the rails after dark.

The 1960s saw one of the area's grisliest tragedies unfold. It occurred as a teenage couple was walking along a scenic overlook. As they were taking in the sights, the boy suddenly lost his footing, sending him tumbling headfirst down the rocky embankment.

It was all over in a matter of seconds. Everything went deathly quiet as the girl leaned forward, uncertain of what she would see. The horror that met her eyes was worse than anything she could have imagined.

Amid the tangled overgrowth, she could see the twisted body of her boyfriend. After shouting his name and receiving no response, she ran for help. Emergency personnel arrived as quickly as possible, but there was no hope of saving the boy who had died either on impact or shortly thereafter.

As his body was being removed from the scene, the hysterical girl could see that the boy's scalp had been torn away, revealing the skull underneath. His face, too, had been mangled so severely that he was nearly unrecognizable.

The girl was so traumatized by the sight that she couldn't form a coherent sentence when questioned about the events of the day. The nightmare she witnessed would haunt, not only her, but the site where the accident occurred for years to come.

Following the boy's untimely death, visitors to the locale complained that, while trying to enjoy the breathtaking view, they had been overcome by a crushing feeling of sadness and despair as they stood atop the overlook.

The casualties continued when, a few months after the boy's death, two teenagers were struck and killed on the nearby train tracks. A rash of suicides also took place around this time. Inexplicably, this quiet place, steeped in the beauty of nature, possessed a dark undercurrent that prompted people with no history of depression to impulsively take their own lives.

In the 1990s, a woman and her young son met an oncoming train while attempting to cross a bridge. The mother managed to push the child to safety just prior to impact. The youngster survived, but his devoted mother did not. The train's engineer, who had tried in vain to avoid the accident, retrieved the five-year-old from beneath the overpass and comforted him until help arrived.

The road once known as Lawler Ford Road is now called Rock Hollow Trail, aka, Al Foster Trail. No longer a viable route, it is utilized these days as a tourist attraction. Accessible only during daylight hours, its "creep factor" is said to be off the charts.

This location, home to an Native American burial ground, a zombie who also happens to be a serial killer, Satanists, demons, ghosts and who knows what else, is a small slice of St. Louis County that offers up an urban legend and then some. Sometimes, it is the most glorious looking of places that harbor the darkest secrets.

Chapter 33:
The Elevator Man

There are few among us who haven't paused for a moment before stepping onto an elevator with someone who makes us feel uneasy. In most cases, we ignore our instincts; concluding that the suspicious character is harmless. Usually, we are right.

In the opposite scenario, we are joined by someone who follows us onto the lift. We inch away as they stand much too close, prompting an involuntary shiver. When we finally reach our stop, we hop off, relieved that the uncomfortable ordeal is over. This is what normally happens in real-life, but not necessarily how events progress in the terrifying urban legend known as "The Elevator Man."

This one begins with a woman leaving work after a long day. The last one to depart for the evening, she gets on the elevator and pushes the button for the fourth floor where she has to pick up a few items before heading home for the night. Just as the doors are about to close, a man appears out of nowhere and joins her. Surprised that someone else is still in the building, she nods politely; a gesture that is not returned.

As he leans forward and presses a button, the woman sees that the man's destination is the level below hers. Well-groomed and wearing an expensive tailored suit, the man cuts quite a figure. The two of them stand at opposite ends of the elevator as they wait for it to stop on the third floor.

The lift comes to a halt and the bell dings indicating that the doors are about to open. As they do, the man turns to the woman and opens his overcoat revealing a large knife that is tucked away in the inner pocket. He then steps out into the hallway. Glancing back as the doors begin to close, he smiles and says "See you soon."

The woman realizes immediately that it is too late to abort the impending stop on the fourth floor. She knows that the man has more than likely used the stairs to beat her to the upcoming stop. The terrifying reality of what awaits her when the doors open begins to sink in as her mind races to find a way out of the predicament.

A split-second later, the familiar ping signals the end of the ride. As the doors slowly open, her eyes meet those of the stranger. As he moves forward, blocking her exit, the man raises the knife high above his head. The woman's screams echo in the empty corridor as her world suddenly goes dark.

Playing into our primal fear of being trapped with someone who means to do us harm, this one hits home with a lot of people. Although there are no cases on record that exactly match the aforementioned incident, that doesn't mean that such an event is impossible.

One disturbing example occurred in a Brooklyn housing project in 2014. It was on a sunny June day that a seven-year old girl and a six-year-old boy set out for a local park. After several hours spent playing under the hot sun, the two decided that it was time to take a break.

Tired and hungry, they ran back to the building where they both lived in order to grab some snacks. They had planned to return to the park after retrieving some freezer pops, but never made it.

When the children entered the elevator that led to their families' apartments, they were joined by a man who got on right after them. As they laughed and jabbered, as youngsters do, the other rider ordered them to be quiet.

On the heels of his harsh command, the man pulled out an eight-inch knife. In the harrowing moments that followed, he repeatedly stabbed both children. The girl, who suffered sixteen penetrating wounds, miraculously survived. The young boy was not so lucky.

Neighbors heard the screams and quickly came to the aid of the brutalized youngsters. Their assailant had fled, but not before being seen by numerous witnesses. He was apprehended four days later thanks to their detailed descriptions.

The man who had killed the six-year-old and critically injured the little girl had a long history of criminal behavior. He would later admit that he had deliberately followed the children that day. In their innocence, they had been oblivious to the fact that they were being watched.

The suspect, Daniel St. Hubert was convicted in 2018 on counts of murder and attempted murder. The surviving victim, who was eleven years old at the time of the trial, testified against her assailant. Just she had on the day of the attack; she referred to him as "the bad man."

Elevators also have a reputation as places where horrible, disfiguring accidents often occur. Although they are hardly commonplace, these events aren't entirely unheard of. One memorable incident involved a surgical resident named Dr. Hitoshi Nikaidoh.

The shocking freak accident took place in Houston, Texas in 2003 when the busy young physician rushed to catch an elevator as the doors were closing. When he reached the lift, he stepped forward, thinking that he could still make it inside. Unfortunately, only his head had crossed the threshold as the doors shut tightly around his neck.

One would think that the mechanisms, sensing that something was caught between them, would have been programmed to automatically open. That did not happen in this case. As a result, what followed was something out of a midnight horror movie.

There is no delicate way of saying that, as the elevator rose to the next level, Nikaidoh's body remained behind. To make a gruesome situation even worse, the elevator had stalled, leaving the lone occupant trapped with the severed head as maintenance crews scrambled to get things up and running.

The odds of someone losing a limb, or worse, in an elevator mishap are remote. Still, as in the case of the doomed Dr. Nikaidoh, sometimes fate has plans for us that defy probability.

It is safe to say that The Elevator Man is probably the product of someone's imagination, but "the bad man" encountered by two children one summer's day was all-too real. Even so, it is extremely unlikely that we will meet our maker at the hands of a stranger we share space with on an elevator.

While that may be true, the thought that such things can happen are enough to make one opt to take the stairs. Of course, they too are legendary hiding places for all sorts of evils, but those are stories for another time and place.

Chapter 34:
Tanning Bed Terror

Tanning booths are bad for those who use them for a variety of reasons. Baking under ultra-violet lights might not be everyone's cup of tea, but for some, they are a routine part of their weekly regime and have been for decades.

After their popularity rose in the late 1970s, these coffin-like devices became the perfect fodder for purveyors of urban legends. This one, known as the "Tanning Bed Terror" has been circulating since the 1980s when the fad was in full swing.

It begins with a woman who is preparing for a big life event, usually her wedding day. Wanting everything to be perfect, she decides that a honey-golden tan would be just the thing to offset her glorious white gown.

When the bride-to-be consults with the proprietor of a local salon, she learns that it will take several sessions in order to achieve the desired hue. That was all well and good except for the fact that they had a cap off of two appointments per week.

With the nuptials only a few days away, the woman knew that she would need more time to reach her goal. Since changing the wedding date wasn't an option, she found a way around the strict tanning bed regulations.

The prospective bride went ahead and took the two sessions available at her regular salon. She then made appointments at every parlor in town that offered the service. On some days, she would tan at several different locations in the span of a few hours. No one seemed to be the wiser as she dashed from one shop to another soaking up the artificial rays.

After the first couple of sessions, the woman started feeling a bit under the weather. Chalking it up to nerves, she continued preparing for the big day in spite of the churning sensation that was taking place inside of her stomach.

By the fourth day, she was unable to keep down a single bite of food. Still, her declining health didn't get in the way of her tanning booth appointments. It was while partaking in one of the many sessions she had lined up on the day before her wedding that things took a turn for the worse.

While lying between the lamps, she suddenly became violently ill. Smoke began to seep from her nose and mouth as blood oozed from every orifice. Within seconds, her body shut down and her heart stopped beating. The owner of the establishment was the one who discovered the decimated body when she came to inform her client that her time was up.

An autopsy showed that the woman's internal organs had been exposed to an excessive amount of heat. The coroner had never seen anything like it. In his expert opinion, the body lying before him had been cooked from the inside out.

In another variation, the woman makes it to her wedding in spite of suffering from agonizing stomach pains. The groom is the first to notice an odd smell that seems to be emanating from his new bride. The nauseating stench reminds him of overcooked meat.

The woman's worsening condition, coupled with the odor, prompts the couple to make a stop at the emergency room before embarking on their honeymoon. Extensive tests reveal the shocking news that not only have her organs been baked, but that they are now in an advanced state of spoilage.

These stories are outlandish, to be sure. After all, tanning beds are not microwave ovens. They tan the outer layer of skin using intense UV rays that mimic those produced naturally by the sun. Heat lamps are not known to penetrate the inner workings of the body.

Microwaves, on the other hand, expose food to electromagnetic radiation that causes the polar molecules found inside to rotate and produce their own thermal energy. The friction that builds up results in a faster cooking time than that which can be achieved by conventional cooking methods.

That being said, there is a real story behind this legend. It begins in Portage, Indiana with a woman who thought she was following doctor's orders. The end result would be almost as disturbing as the ones depicted in the previous tales.

Forty-five-year-old Patsy Campbell had suffered from psoriasis for much of her life. The itchy skin condition had led her to seek medical help on more than one occasion to no avail. In 1989, she met with someone who finally offered her a glimmer of hope.

The osteopath prescribed the medication psoralen as a first step in her treatment plan. According to Patsy's family, a tanning bed regime had also been approved as part of her therapy. Patsy hoped that if she followed the physician's recommended protocol, she might someday be psoriasis-free.

Eager to get the ball rolling on the much-anticipated treatments, Patsy made a tanning bed appointment at a reputable beauty salon. On her first visit, she spent twenty-five minutes under the lamps. As she prepared to leave, she noticed an intense burning sensation all over, but assumed that it was due to her body's adjusting to the artificial rays.

Within a matter of days, burns covered almost every inch of Patsy's skin. She was rushed to the emergency room where her condition was deemed too grave to be treated locally. Transferred to the burn unit at the University of Chicago, Patsy would succumb to systemic infection eleven days later.

An investigation was launched which concluded that the psoralen, which causes hyper sensitivity to light, had reacted with the ultraviolet rays resulting in the burns that would ultimately claim Patsy's life. Even though she had followed her doctor's orders to the letter, the combination of treatments had caused her skin to bake in the intense heat.

Patsy's family sued the doctor who had recommended the unorthodox combination of treatments. In 1991, the Indiana State Medical Review Board found that the osteopath had been negligent in her care of Patsy Campbell.

It was rumored that the tanning bed involved in the incident had to be removed from service and placed in storage. It seemed that anyone who laid in it for the same amount of time as Patsy—twenty-five minutes—would suffer excruciating burns that mimicked hers. Unlike Patsy, these victims were not taking any medications that would account for such extreme reactions.

In 2014, the tanning bed was allegedly added to the database of Warehouse 13 which collects information on items suspected of being cursed or otherwise tainted. It remains there today, filed away with other supernatural artifacts.

Tanning beds are not the healthiest thing one can expose their body to, but neither are they human slow cookers. For those who insist on showing off that sun-kissed glow, the benefits outweigh the dangers.

Of course, there are the rare cases, like Patsy's, where a perfect storm of circumstances allow the unthinkable to occur. Her tragic story was, indeed, a tanning bed terror.

Chapter 35:
Slaughterhouse Canyon

The gold rush of the 1800s was fraught with unexplained deaths and disappearances. It seemed that in their frenzy to strike it rich, many prospectors threw caution to the wind, often with tragic results. One of these mysterious vanishings would lay the groundwork for Arizona's most infamous urban legend.

In 1858, gold was discovered in the area around the Gila River, about twenty miles from the town of Yuma. Word of the find spread like wildfire, prompting dozens of families to uproot and move to the desolate canyons of Arizona.

As the women stayed behind and tended to the children, the men would spend their days panning for hidden riches. These long-suffering wives would be left alone with their young ones, sometimes, for days or weeks on end as their husbands mined the land.

As legend has it, one such family moved to a remote area they christened Luana's Canyon in honor of their matriarch. It was she who would be the catalyst for a tale that would be passed down through the ages.

The events that would alter their lives forever began innocently enough one morning when Luana's spouse set off on another of his many attempts to find the gold that had so far eluded him. It should have been an outing like any other, but this time would be different. They didn't know as they exchanged parting words that these would be their final goodbyes.

Days turned to weeks as Luana waited for her husband to return. As she pondered his fate, the idea invaded her mind that, perhaps, he had hit the mother lode and decided to abandon her and their two children. She also wondered if he had fallen victim to the human scavengers who were said to roam the gorges, killing miners and reaping their rewards. The possibilities preyed on her subconscious as she tried her best to hold it together for her children.

As the gravity of her situation took hold; Luana's worries began to multiply. The most pressing of these was the family's slowly dwindling food supply. As rations got dangerously low, an ever-growing panic overwhelmed her. With no means of finding sustenance, a hunger set in that gnawed away, not only on Luana's stomach, but also her psyche.

Left on her own with a cabin full of hungry mouths to feed, the young mother's mental state deteriorated with each tick of the clock. The pressure inside of her built up until she finally snapped.

As her children cried and begged for food, as they had done for days, their mother calmly walked to the trunk in which she stored her wedding dress. After donning the garment, she picked up an axe that was propped near the fireplace and systematically hacked both of her offspring to death. Afterwards, Luana took her own life; putting an end to her suffering and that of her children once and for all.

An alternate version holds that after committing the murders, Luana chopped up the bodies and threw the pieces into the nearby river. She then walked into the water and kept going until it was over her head. It was there that she drowned, surrounded by her family's dismembered remains.

Some say that the mother, by then quite mad, couldn't bring herself to take her own life. Instead, she stayed in the cabin, slowly wasting away from the ravages of starvation and exposure.

The family's cabin, which was little more than a shack, was destroyed long ago. Reminders of the events thought to have occurred there, however, live on to this day. Among them are the cries of Luana's children that have been heard echoing throughout the canyon. The pitiful sobs turn to screams, presumably as they are confronted by their axe-wielding mother.

The night winds are also rumored to carry the tortured sounds of that fateful day, long ago, when the lives of the children were brutally ended. When the deed is done, a brief silence settles over the land for a few seconds, often followed by the mournful wails of Luana as she comes to terms with her actions.

The legend of the miner's wife, driven to madness and murder by the suffering of her loved ones, has been around for over a century. There is no way of knowing how accurate the account of the doomed family really is, but it does have its roots in actual events.

Visitors to the area, especially after dark, claim that they have heard the sounds of the family's agonizing final moments reverberating through the place now known as Slaughterhouse Canyon. Located twelve miles outside of the town of Kingman, the tourist attraction is open to those curious souls who wish to find out the truth for themselves.

Chapter 36:
The Open Grave

The stage for this eerie urban legend is a cemetery where there happens to be a freshly dug, unoccupied, grave. Of course, it doesn't stay that way for long.

The story begins with a gravedigger who has spent the afternoon preparing a final resting place for a fellow whose funeral is scheduled to take place the following morning. Gazing overhead, he sees that ominous black clouds are beginning to gather in the sky. He finishes up quickly, hoping to get home ahead of the impending storm.

Normally, he would have taken a few minutes to cover the gaping hole he had created, but on this day, he is too tired to bother with what is, in his view, a minor detail. Besides, he tells himself, what is the worst that could happen?

In his haste to outrun the tempest he knows is coming, he neglects to secure the gate on his way out. Soon after his departure, the entire cemetery is blanketed in darkness as the first drops of rain begin to fall.

Sometime well past midnight, two men leaving a bar on foot accidently veer off the street and end up in the cemetery. As the rain beats down upon them, they wander among the tombstones, too inebriated to recognize their surroundings.

At some point, one of them slips in the mud and tumbles into the grave that had been dug a few hours earlier. He claws at the dirt in an attempt to climb back up to solid ground, but his advanced state of drunkenness, coupled with the rain-soaked earth, make it impossible for him to get a foothold.

After a few minutes of trying to free himself from the confines of the grave, the man gives up the struggle. Adopting the attitude of "If you can't beat them, join them," he lies down in the wet dirt and falls fast asleep.

While his friend dozes peacefully in the ground, the other drunkard leans against a headstone as he contemplates his next move. Gathering the few senses he has left, he staggers off in search of his drinking buddy. Unable to maintain his balance, he falls headfirst into the open plot now occupied by his companion.

The impact rouses the one who is sleeping, causing him to momentarily rise to a sitting position. The other man instantly sobers up; certain that he has awakened a corpse. Panic erupts as the men fight to free themselves from each other's grasp.

Empowered by fear, the second man manages to scale the muddy walls of the grave. The fate of his friend varies depending on who's telling the story. Sometimes, he finds his way out as soon as the rain lets up.

In other accounts, he drifts into such a deep sleep that no one is aware of his presence. Morning comes and members of the staff notice that the grave is partially filled with water. This comes as no surprise to them since it had rained throughout the night.

The workers had not observed anything unusual when they inspected the grave. The depth of the hole made it difficult to see the bottom clearly. As a result, they had overlooked the figure, passed out and half-covered in rainwater, who lay in the burial site.

The funeral proceeds right on schedule. As the casket is lowered into the ground, no one hears the muffled cries of the man who awakens just as the crushing weight pushes him deeper into the mud. The final prayers are uttered as mourners say their last goodbyes. As they file out, one by one, none of them realize that two bodies were buried that day.

The man who was unintentionally interred on that overcast morning was reported missing by his wife later on the same day. Since he was never heard from again, it was assumed that he had wandered off to parts unknown to begin life anew. Sadly, his family would live out their lives never knowing the truth.

The idea that cemetery personnel would neglect to notice someone snoozing in an open grave is a stretch, to be sure. There have, however, been instances in which people have fallen into plots and not been discovered until it was too late. One such incident made the back pages of newspapers worldwide when it occurred in Portugal in 2017.

Fifty-six-year-old Manuel Gomes was a gravedigger by trade. An employee of the Freixo Cemetery since his youth, Gomes was a hard worker who took his position more seriously than most. For him, preparing resting places for the recently deceased was an honorable duty not to be taken lightly.

On the last day of his life, Gomes had been digging away when he was suddenly overcome by a dizzy spell. As the world around him began to spin, he fell forward into the plot he was in the process of excavating.

Gomes was out cold by the time he landed in the soft dirt. He would lay there for several hours before his body was discovered by a passerby who happened to notice Gomes' work implements strewn about. Curious, they had glanced down into the freshly dug grave. What they saw sent them running for help.

Emergency responders were on the scene as quickly as possible. They rushed to pull Gomes to the surface, careful not to cause any further harm. Paramedics knew as soon as they examined the body that there was nothing they could do. Manuel Gomes, his skin cold to the touch and his eyes unseeing, was past needing medical attention.

It was later determined that Gomes' heart had given out, causing him to lose consciousness. The coroner felt that death had soon followed, but he couldn't be certain how long Gomes had lived after falling into the grave.

Those who knew him in life prayed that Gomes passed with no knowledge of his dire situation. The thought that he may have awoken to find himself trapped underground with no way out was not something anyone wanted to contemplate. Hopefully, he slipped away peacefully, never knowing that, for a short time, he alone lay breathing among hundreds who breathed no more.

Chapter 37:
Mandy

No collection of urban legends would be complete without a story that revolves around a cursed doll. These tales are plentiful, but few are as well-documented as that of Mandy, a porcelain baby doll that not only resembles a human child, but behaves like one as well.

The events that would lead to the doll's discovery are thought to have taken place in Europe in the early 1900s. It all started when a man out for a walk in the countryside passed by an abandoned farmhouse.

As he strolled along, taking in the scenery, he heard the sound of a child crying in the distance. Curiosity got the better of him and he made a detour onto the property. "No Trespassing" signs were posted all around, but he didn't let that stop him as he made his way through the weeds that led to the front porch.

The closer he got to the house, the louder the crying became. It was clear to him that the noises weren't originating from the main level of the dilapidated shack, but from someplace underground.

Once he spotted the cellar doors, he knew what he had to do. Kicking away the debris that was blocking his access, the man pulled open the doors that led to the depths of the house. With only a beam of sunlight to guide him, he made his way down the homemade ladder that substituted for stairs.

The man hadn't yet reached the floor when something caught his eye. Amid the filth, her arms clasped tightly around a doll, lay the body of a young girl. The child, who looked to be no more than six or seven years old, had been well-preserved in the dank cellar. He couldn't tell by the state of her remains how long she had lain, forgotten, in the darkness.

He would later tell his wife that he was convinced that the pitiful cries that led him to the discovery had come, not from the child, but from the doll. Whereas the little girl seemed to be at peace, her companion's face had been a mask of hostility. It had given him such a horrible feeling that he had hurried back up the ladder, shutting the doors behind him. The man knew that no normal toy would wear such a frightening expression.

The body of the deceased girl was removed from the premises, along with the doll that had kept her company for who knows how long. It turned out that the last family known to have lived in the house had moved out of the area years before the body was found.

The girl was never identified nor was her cause of death ever conclusively determined. One possibility put forth was that she had found her way onto the property and accidentally fallen into the cellar while playing. Hitting her head on the way down, she passed away on the dirt floor. The fact that no one had come looking for her or reported her missing made this scenario unlikely.

Another theory was that she had been an unwanted member of the family that had previously occupied the house. It was rumored that the girl's punishment for misbehaving involved being locked in the cellar, sometimes for days on end, without food or water. When her parents were satisfied that she had learned her lesson, they would allow her to rejoin the family.

At some point, the parents gave up on their child. As a result, she waited in the pitch black cellar for a reprieve that would never come. Instead, she died alone with only her doll to keep her company.

After finding their daughter's body, her parents packed up their remaining children and fled in the middle of the night. No one knew where they went or what became of them. In time, perhaps they erased their daughter's memory from their minds. The one that comforted her in her final hours would, however, never forget.

A funeral was held for the girl, attended mostly by people who had never known her in life. The doll changed hands several times over the years, eventually ending up in Canada.

The doll would become known to the public in 1991 when it was gifted to a museum in British Columbia. The donor, a woman named Mereanda, told the curator that, even though the doll had been in her family for decades, she no longer wished to be responsible for the valuable antique.

Known to the family as Mandy, the doll showed obvious signs of wear. The glass eyes and wisps of blonde hair that peeked out from beneath a knit cap were offset by an assortment of cracks that marred her delicate features.

The curator surmised that the doll was approaching a hundred years old, probably having been made around 1910-1920. Even in her less-than-perfect condition, Mandy was considered a treasure. Mereanda was relieved that the doll had found a new home. She left that day confidant that she had done the right thing, not only for her family, but for Mandy.

As was customary for new arrivals, Mandy had to be sealed in airtight plastic on the off-chance that she carried parasites. No artifacts could be displayed without going through this process.

Staff members in charge of placing the doll in the holding bag claimed that they heard rustling noises soon after. When the quarantine was over, no bugs or other pests were detected. No one could account for the movement they had all seen and heard taking place within the virtually impenetrable sack.

Another of the museum's policies called for items to be meticulously photographed as a way of documenting their condition. Upon completion of Mandy's photoshoot, she was left in the lab overnight. The next morning, workers arrived to find the room in shambles. Objects that had been in their rightful places at lights out had been thrown on the floor sometime after closing.

They also noted that much of the equipment had been either knocked over or shifted from one area to another. Many of the apparatuses were considered too heavy to have been moved by a single person.

It wasn't long after her arrival that Mandy's personality quirks began to manifest. It was discovered that anytime she was left unattended in a room, the place would be wrecked within a matter of minutes. The destruction was likened to the aftermath of a child's uncontrolled temper tantrum.

Papers left out on desks would be tossed haphazardly onto the floor. Pens and pencils would be missing, never to be recovered. Other objects destined for the showroom would be found smashed to pieces if they were kept anywhere near Mandy.

The doll ultimately made her way to the public display cases. Once there, her activity only grew in momentum. Visitors often relate the experience of taking photos of Mandy only to have them appear either blurry or completely blacked out. It is noted that other pictures taken on the same day, using the same devices, show no such flaws.

Patrons and staff alike tell of seeing the doll's eyes blink spontaneously. Her head is also said to turn as if she is keeping a close watch on all who are present. Likewise, the doll's body has been known to change positions even though she is secured behind glass.

Resting inside of her enclosed space, Mandy holds a toy lamb on her lap. On several occasions, the stuffed animal has been found lying outside of the case even though the latch remains in place.

The museum's curator found it increasingly difficult to ignore the phenomena surrounding Mandy. Determined to get to the bottom of things, she paid a visit to the previous owner. When confronted with the behaviors attributed to the doll; Mereanda finally came clean.

She admitted that her claim that she had donated the doll because she feared that her young daughter might damage it had been only partially true. In reality, she had come to believe that Mandy was more than just a manufactured toy. Mereanda had seen and heard things that convinced her that something inside of the doll was alive.

Mereanda told the curator that there were times when she would hear crying coming from her storm shelter. When she went to investigate, she would find Mandy sitting alone in the underground room. Taking into account that she was the only one at the time who had access to the doll, there was no logical explanation for Mandy's presence in the cellar.

Mereanda stated that the mournful crying ceased when Mandy was removed from the house for good. She never heard it again. A sense of peace she had not known for years had found her once the doll was no longer a part of the family.

An avid collector, Mereanda boasted a large array of dolls from all over the world. She learned early on that Mandy could not be kept anywhere near the others. Anytime she made the mistake of placing a new acquisition close to Mandy, she would later find it in ruins. The curator could relate. Mandy's jealous streak was well-known to the employees of the museum.

Mereanda ended up confining the doll to the area of the house where she could do the least amount of damage; the basement. It was there that Mandy remained until the day she was handed over to the museum. It was one of the best decisions Mereanda had ever made.

As of January, 2020, Mandy remains on display at the Quesnel Museum in British Columbia. She remains a force to be reckoned with, if accounts are to be believed. A psychic brought in to examine Mandy determined that she retains the spirit of an abused child.

From what the medium could gather, the young girl had died as a result of neglect. As her life ebbed away, she had willed her soul into the body of the doll. Once trapped inside, the child's essence had become one with the inanimate object.

The story of Mandy began in an old farmhouse with the discovery of a dead child and her doll. With the passage of time, the events faded from the memories of all those involved. All that is, except for Mandy and the soul said to reside inside of her porcelain facade.

If the psychic's reading was accurate then Mandy is more than just a cursed object with the ability to act out at will. She is a child who still hungers for the attention she never received in life. Today, as the object of fascination for throngs of visitors, Mandy is at last the center of attention.

Chapter 38:
Nain Rouge

The city of Detroit, sometimes called 'The Paris of the Midwest,' is famous for more than rock music and a once booming auto industry. One of its most lasting legacies comes in the form of a demon said to have laid a curse upon the metropolis centuries ago, the effects of which are still being felt today.

In 1701, the city's founder was out enjoying his nightly stroll along the tree-lined streets of his neighborhood. From out of the darkness, a monstrous figure emerged. Although small in stature, it carried itself in such an aggressive manner that the man lifted his cane and struck the interloper several times.

The would-be attacker was stunned, but otherwise uninjured. It was only when it stood in the moonlight that the man got his first good look at the tiny form. He would later describe what he saw as being completely red from head to toe, around three-feet tall and sporting the cloven hooves and horns of a devil.

Directing its anger towards the man wielding the wooden staff, what would come to be known as "Nain Rouge," or "Red Dwarf," began reciting words that the founder didn't understand. When it was finished saying its peace, it disappeared into the night.

The man would relate his experience to his family who worried that he might have suffered some sort of mental episode. After all, they reasoned, such a preposterous event couldn't actually have occurred. They told him this so often, in fact, that he became convinced that he had imagined the entire episode.

Not long after the man's encounter with the Nain Rouge, residents began reporting run-ins with an old man who had a fiery red face, gleaming eyes and a mouthful of snaggleteeth. Even though he had only stood a couple of feet tall, the man had struck fear in all who crossed his path.

In time, a pattern emerged suggesting that anytime the Nain Rouge was spotted, tragedy would soon follow. In 1763, he was seen near the banks of the Detroit River. A few days later, the Battle of Bloody Run was fought. Fifty-eight British soldiers lay dead once the smoke cleared.

As decades past, it was accepted as a given that the Nain Rouge was both a messenger of doom and, in some cases, the cause of that which he heralded. To see him meant that death and destruction were not far away.

In 1805, fire decimated the city following a visit from the Nain Rouge. He had also been witnessed scaling a utility pole in the days before an ice storm ravaged the area in 1976. City workers were the first to catch sight of the red menace. Not fully understanding what they had seen, they reported it as having been a child making the dangerous climb.

During times of war, the Nain Rouge was not afraid to insert himself front and center. In the midst of the War of 1812, General William Hull surrendered Fort Detroit with little more than a whimper. Hull was ultimately court-martialed and sentenced to death for his act of cowardice.

In his defense, he claimed that a red demon had controlled his decision-making process. According to him, he had been compelled to act on the orders laid out for him by the devilish creature.

President Madison commuted Hull's sentence to life, sparing him from execution. Whether the Nain Rouge had truly orchestrated the surrender of the fort, or if Hull made the whole thing up to cover his lack of leadership skills is a question that will forever remain unanswered.

The Red Dwarf was said to have been seen wandering the streets in advance of the riots of 1967. On that occasion, Forty-three people were killed over the course of five days as violence erupted between police and citizens.

The citizens of Detroit believe so strongly in the power of the Nain Rouge that they hold a parade every spring dedicated to keeping him out of their city. As part of the festivities, the Red Dwarf is burned in effigy. The act is intended to warn the troublesome imp to stay away lest he be subjected to the same.

Revelers are invited to come dressed in costumes, but are cautioned to not wear the same attire two years in a row. To do so makes the offender identifiable to the Nain Rouge who is said to observe the festivities from afar.

On top of being a harbinger of doom, the demon also has a reputation for holding a grudge. If he feels wronged, he will waste no time exacting his revenge. To get on his bad side almost never ends well for the other party.

The bad blood between the Nain Rouge and the city of Detroit is thought to have its origins in that fateful beatdown that occurred in 1701. According to legend, a fortune teller had warned the founder of his impending encounter with the Red Dwarf. She told him not to fear. The devilish character, although intimidating at first, had only the best of intentions.

To befriend Nain Rouge, she said, would bring good fortune to the city in perpetuity. She was quick to add that, to insult him in any way would turn his bonhomie to vengeance. She cautioned that, once his wrath was incurred, there would be no going back.

Even though he had been schooled in how to treat the Nain Rouge, the city's founder had panicked in the moment and attacked the imp. As a result, he set in motion a curse that stands to this day. Evidently, a demon that comes in peace and is turned away never forgets—or forgives.

Chapter 39:
The Roommate

This last offering is included solely for its creep factor. No documented cases could be found that laid a foundation for the story, but neither is there anything that definitively proves it to be false.

The tale unfolds in a college dormitory where two young women, Karen and Jamie, are preparing for finals. In the middle of their study session, Jamie's boyfriend stops by and persuades her to accompany him to a party. He doesn't have to ask twice. At her wits' end from hours spent with her head buried in textbooks, she is more than happy to call it a day.

The couple invites Karen to join them, but she declines. The dedicated student sees them out before once again immersing herself in her studies. As minutes turn to hours, the exhausted young woman finally decides to turn in as the clock strikes twelve. Assuming that Jamie has opted to spend the night someplace else, she turns off the lights and collapses in bed.

Jamie returns to the room a couple of hours later. Having consumed a bit more alcohol than she can handle, she fumbles around in the dark, careful not to wake her sleeping roommate.

Making her way to the bedroom, she quietly tucks in. In less than fifteen minutes, she has drifted off to dreamland. She sleeps peacefully, unaware of the terror morning will bring.

Jamie is awakened several hours later when the first light of day beams into her room. Half-hungover, she shuffles towards the kitchenette. As she is passing through the living area, she notices that the place is in a state of disarray.

When her eyes focus, she sees that a chair has been knocked over. Beside it, pieces of a shattered lamp lay strewn about the floor. Knowing what a neat freak Karen can be, she can't imagine why she would have gone to bed without cleaning up the mess.

With classes set to begin in less than an hour, Jamie taps on her roomies bedroom door. Receiving no answer, she opens it a crack and informs Karen that it's time to get up. With the blinds closed, Jamie can't make out anything in the room. Stepping across the threshold, she flips on the overhead light.

Jamie stifles a scream as her eyes survey the scene before her. The first thing she sees is Karen lying sideways across the bed. Her head is hanging off the edge, revealing a gaping wound to her throat. Jamie doesn't have to check for signs of life; she can tell by the state of Karen's body that it would be pointless.

As she looks around the room, desperate for answers, she sees something on the wall adjacent to the mirror. There, written in blood, are the taunting words, "Aren't you glad you didn't turn on the lights?"

Realizing that the message was left for her, Jamie finally releases the scream she has been suppressing.

The alternate version begins much the same way, with two girls hard at work studying for an upcoming exam. Knowing that she will be burning the midnight oil, the more diligent of the pair packs up her notes and heads to the basement study hall.

Around two o'clock in the morning, she realizes that she is missing one of her textbooks. She goes upstairs and lets herself into the shared dorm room. Since no lights are on, she assumes that her roommate has gone to bed.

As she tiptoes in the dark, she notices a strange metallic smell that permeates the living room. Although it's familiar to her, she can't quite place the pungent odor. Thinking that her roommate may have cooked something that was past expiration, she proceeds with the task at hand.

After a few minutes spent feeling her way in the dark, she finds the elusive tome. As she steps into the hallway, closing the door behind her, gooseflesh rises on her arms. She knows instinctively that something isn't right, but talks herself out of going back to investigate. It would turn out to be the wisest decision she had ever made.

The girl returns to the basement where she continues to study straight through till dawn. Realizing that class time is fast approaching, she makes her way up to her room with the intention of grabbing a shower and, if time permits, a quick nap.

She knows as soon as she opens the door that she will not be making it to class that day. Her roommate's body lay sprawled out in front of the sofa, her throat splayed wide open. Words were scrawled in blood on every wall, indicating that the killer was still in the room when she had come searching for her textbook.

She runs into the hallway and calls out for help before collapsing on the floor. The memories come flooding back of the nauseating stench and the goosebumps that had risen for no apparent reason. The girl is struck with the realization that her efforts to sneak in without waking her roommate had probably saved her life.

The story may not be based on actual events, but that doesn't make it any less frightening. Psychopaths exist in the world, of that we can be sure. They can be anyone, including our next door neighbor or the blind date that seems too good to be true.

The moral of this urban legend is simple: trust your instincts. If the hair suddenly stands up on the back of your neck or your skin prickles for no obvious reason, it might just be your body's defense mechanisms kicking in. You'd be wise to take heed. After all, the gazelle doesn't wait until the lion is upon it to run—that is, unless it chooses to ignore the signal that danger is only a breath away.

Chapter 40:
Love Rollercoaster

In 1975, the Ohio Players had a number one hit with a song called "Love Rollercoaster." While the tune itself was catchy to be sure, it was something that could be heard in the background that would capture the attention of audiences worldwide, and keep them guessing for decades to come.

As anyone who has heard the funk classic can attest, during a four second instrumental break that begins at the 1:24 mark, a piercing scream suddenly erupts in the background. Though faint, the unexpected sound, whether added deliberately or by accident, got tongues wagging.

When the song hit the airwaves, listeners wasted no time lighting up the phone lines with theories as to the nature of the eerie shriek. With a curious public itching for answers, a disc jockey in California decided to give them what they wanted. Seizing the moment, he spun a tale that would eventually snowball into an urban legend.

The story he related involved a murder that had supposedly taken place in the studio on the day the song was being recorded. Numerous variations of what exactly happened made the rounds over the years, making it difficult to pinpoint the original. Regardless, they all centered on the notion that a woman was either horribly injured or killed as the band played on.

One popular theory held that Ester Corbet, the model who appears on the cover of the album on which "Love Rollercoaster" is featured, was the source of the scream.

As the story goes, a nude Ms. Corbet was asked to drizzle warm honey on her body during the shoot to highlight the name of the record, which was—as it happened—*Honey*.

She obliged without realizing that the sugary substance had been overheated. Consequently, it scalded her skin on contact, causing her to cry out in pain. Lore has it that her scream was so loud that it was picked up by the microphones in the recording booth. When the sound engineers discovered the disruption on playback, they opted to leave it in, figuring that no one would notice.

Another unsubstantiated rumor suggested that the blood-curdling screech was that of a woman who was murdered by her jealous beau, a technician who worked at the studio. Apparently, the two had gotten into an argument while the band was busy recording. In the heat of the moment, the man had pulled out a knife and stabbed his girlfriend in a fit of rage.

In an alternate version of events, the victim was a cleaning lady who was killed by a prowler. In other variations, she was either a woman who had gotten into an altercation with a member of the production team, or a clerical worker who was murdered by an unknown assailant who fled before anyone realized that a crime had taken place. In these instances, the woman's body isn't found until much later. Due to the delay, no one notices that her scream was captured on tape until it's too late to rerecord the track.

As speculation whirled around the song, no one took advantage of its notoriety more than the Ohio Players themselves. Realizing that they had been handed a gift that would keep on giving, rather than attempting to set the record straight, they fanned the flames by staying tight-lipped on the subject.

When asked about the nature of the scream, band members refused to confirm or deny that it was the result of foul play. Looking back, who could blame them? Although it would have been a hit one way or another, the added bonus of having an unsolved mystery attached gave it a longevity that any performer would kill for—figuratively speaking of course.

Decades would pass before it was revealed that the scream had not come from a woman in distress after all, but from the band's keyboardist Billy Beck. Unaware that he would be igniting a controversy, he had improvised the scream to liven up an instrumental break in the song. This inspired move would go on to elevate "Love Rollercoaster" to legendary status in both the worlds of music and that of urban myths.

Chapter 41:
The Hamburger Man

Sand Hills State Park rests on over eleven acres of land located some six miles north of Hutchinson, Kansas. In addition to its multitude of sand dunes, grassy plains, marshes and lush forests, it is also home to an alleged serial killer with a taste for human flesh known as the "Hamburger Man."

This story has its beginnings in the 1950s when hikers started coming up missing near an area of the park called "Hamburger Hill." When no trace of them could be found, the local rumor mill began churning with tales of a disfigured outcast who was preying on individuals who made the mistake of wandering too far off the trails.

Those who claimed to have known the perpetrator on some level asserted that he was a farmer whose face had been burned away in a house fire. Rather than subject himself to the stares of a morbidly curious public, he retreated to a shanty deep in the woods where few ever ventured. After years of living off the land and never seeing or speaking to another living soul, his self-imposed isolation was said to have driven him mad.

No longer a member of society, he decided to make up his own rules of conduct. His moral code having eroded long ago, he began viewing the hikers who regularly passed by his ramshackle home—which everyone assumed was abandoned— as a source of sustenance waiting to be harvested. Since those who encountered the madman in the woods weren't around to share the details of their ordeal, local gossips were more than happy to do it for them.

The tales they concocted were gruesome, to put it mildly. Supposedly, and they swore this to be true, the degenerate woodsman would stalk his intended victims from afar, waiting until they were well off the beaten path to strike. When he was certain that his target was alone and oblivious to his presence, he would pounce. After subduing them with the butcher knife he always kept handy, he would drag the unconscious victim into his shack where he would dismember them and grind the remains into hamburger meat.

Over the years, accounts of the Hamburger Man's evildoings were prevalent throughout Hutchinson and the neighboring communities. It seemed that nearly everyone had either seen him lurking in the woods or knew someone who had.

Those who fancied themselves experts on the subject claimed that he only hunted in the darkest regions of the forest due to his fear of being ridiculed for his appearance. With this in mind, they advised hikers to search out trails where the sun wasn't obscured by trees. They also stressed the importance of staying in groups, since the Hamburger Man exclusively hunted people who were alone and therefore vulnerable.

This particular anomaly has been described as being half-ghost, half-monster, mostly due to his longevity. Owing to the belief that he has stalked the area around Hamburger Hill for over seventy years, it is assumed that at some point he transitioned from a living menace to one that refused to cease his activities when death came knocking. Rather than giving in to life's inevitable end, he chose to remain in the woods—the only place he had ever belonged.

As one would imagine, there is absolutely no evidence to back up these assertions. Even so, the legend of the Hamburger Man persists, as it has done for decades. So, if you happen to find yourself in Sand Hills State Park and decide to go for a hike, stick to the designated trails and follow the sun. To do otherwise, if the stories have any merit, could land you front and center on the evening's dinner menu.

Chapter 42:
Shtriga

In parts of southern Europe, an urban legend exists that involves a witch who enters homes clandestinely with the intention of partaking of the blood of newborns in order to steal their youth.

Known as Shtrigas, these nocturnal entities assume the guise of moths before going on the prowl. After gaining access to dwellings through open windows and doors left ajar, they search the premises for unattended infants, their unsuspecting parents blissfully unaware of the menace in their midst.

Upon finding their prey fast asleep, they return to their true form and proceed to feed on the tiny cherubs, careful to take only what they need, while leaving enough to sustain the source. When they're finished, they transition once again before leaving the way they came without anyone the wiser.

For their part, the victims are virtually unharmed, at least on the surface. However, the damage that has been done is far greater than anyone could imagine. It seems that for every ounce of precious blood the leech woman consumes, she gains a year of the infant's life yet to come.

In some depictions, the Shtriga is a haggard figure whose appearance is a fright. In others, she is a peerless beauty whose delicate features remain untouched by the ravages of time. Having found the secret to eternal youth, she revels in the envious stares of strangers.

Following a common thread that seems to run through a good deal of urban legends, these witches reside deep in the forest. Their evil deeds kept tightly under wraps, they live for centuries on the time they have stolen from others.

On the rare occasions when one of these heinous beings is caught in the act, she will attempt to make amends by undoing her misdeed. She accomplishes this by placing her lips on those of her victim and regurgitating the blood that was taken, thus restoring the purloined years.

Since the best defense is a good offense, there are ways to keep these nefarious parasites at bay. One tried and true method is to line every entrance with an unbroken trail of salt. It's well-known that witches who are up to no good can't cross the powerful mineral without stopping to count every last grain. When faced with the arduous task, most will move on rather than wasting time that would be better spent searching elsewhere for unwilling donors.

Another means of protection is to hang a cross near the crib or bassinet of sleeping infants. Unable to stand the sight of the holy symbol, the Shtriga will beat a hasty retreat from any space where a cross is prominently displayed.

Last but not least, if you happen to spy a large moth casing your home, lock everything up tight post-haste. After all, it's impossible to know if it's simply a candle fly that has lost its way or a narcissistic witch on a never-ending quest for the fountain of youth.

Acknowledgements

Thank you to my family. You are the ones that matter most, now and forever.

As always, thank you to those who read and hopefully enjoy my work. If not for you, it would all be for naught.

Thank you to whatever force in the universe instilled in me the never-ending desire to open my mind to all possibilities, no matter how outlandish they may seem. The belief that nothing is off-limits sustains me, as I hope it does you.

Resources:

Historic-uk.com
Atlasobscura.com
Monsterfandom.com
buzzfeed.com
pbs.com
thoughtcatalog.com
reddit.com
storymuseum.org.uk
vitalsource.com
ranker.com
reuters.com
motorbiscuit.com
worldhistorycommons.org
medium.com
columbiatribune.com
columbiamissourian.com
slate.com
villains.fandom.com
cnn.com
people.howstuffworks.com
mirrorworld.co.uk
sun-sentinel.com
Nightmares (1983) Jeffrey Bloom and Christopher Crowe
nytimes.com
gothamist.com
nypost.com
Night Gallery (1972) Rod Serling and Oscar Cook
deseret.com
thescientist.com
mancunianmatters.co.uk
mentalfloss.com
atlasobsura.com, ancientorigins.net
Paranormal Guide

Dangerous Roads
St. Louis Magazine
St. Louis Today
The Museum of Hoaxes
ScoopWhoop
Stoneham Studies
The Line-up.com
The Daily Dot
Mother Nature Network
Live About
Wiki
Planet Dolan
Nicaragua Community
El Salvadortips.com
Tees.ac.uk
Abovetopsecret.com
Smithsonian Magazine
BestRide.com
The Vintage News
National Deer Alliance
Tulsa World
Haunted New Orleans Tours
Mysterious Universe
Nightwatch Paranormal
Only in Your State
Urban Legends from Around the World
The History Channel
Offbeat.topix.com
Live Science
Weird U.S.
Brian A. Conley
WAMU

The Washingtonian
Country Living
Listverse
Arkansas Democrat Gazette
Quotev.com
Unexplained Mysteries
Michigan's Otherside
insider.com
songfacts.com
niagara-gazette.com
cleveland19.com
crytidspot.com
toledohistorybox.com
onlyinyourstate.com-Katie Lawrence
1063thebuzz.com
thedallassocials.com
thesunflower.com
ihorror.com
thoughtcatalog.com
onlyinyourstate.com
unnaturalworld.fandom.com
supernaturalwiki.com

Films and Television Related to These Stories

·*Urban Legend* (1998) Directed by Jamie Blanks
·*Urban Legends: Final Cut* (2000) Directed by John Ottman
·*Urban Legends: Bloody Mary* (2005) Directed by Mary Lambert
·*The Bunny Man* (2021) Directed by Bobby McGruther
·*Scary Stories to Tell in the Dark* (2019) Directed by Andre Ovredal
·*Campfire Tales* (1997) Directed by Martin Kunert and David Semel
·*Night Gallery* "The Caterpillar" (1972) Directed by Jeannot Szwarc
·*The Believers* (1987) Directed by John Schlesinger
·*Nightmares* (1983) Directed by Joseph Sargent
·*Alligator* (1980) Directed by Lewis Teague
·*Sewer Alligators* (2022) Directed by Paul Dale
·*Spring-Heeled Jack* (2008) Directed by William Honeyball
·*Spring-Heeled Jack* (2016) Directed by Stephen Corston
·*Hellhounds* (2013) Directed by Eric Widing
·*Mandy the Doll* (2018) Directed by Jamie Weston
·*Close Encounters of the Third Kind* (1977) Directed by Steven Spielberg
·*The Harvest* (1993) Directed by David Marconi
·*Beware the Slenderman* (2016) Directed by Irene Taylor Brodsky
·*Slender Man Stabbing: The Untold Story* (2019) James Buddy Day
·*The Curse of Bucket Road* (2017) Directed by Matthew Currie Holmes
·*Sarajevo* (2014) Directed by Andreas Prochaska
·*Devil's Night: Dawn of Nain Rouge* (2019) Directed by Sam Logan Khaleghi
·*Beast of Bray Road* (2005) Directed by Leigh Scott
·*The Bray Road Beast* (2018) Directed by Seth Breedlove

·*Black Eyed Children: Let Me In* (2015) Directed by Justin Snyder and Serene Tohmy
·*The Black-Eyed Children* (2011) Directed by Matt Matzen
·*Sunshine Girl and the Hunt for Black Eyed Kids* (2012) Directed by Nicholas J. Hagen
·*The Vanishing Hitchhiker* (2016) Short Directed by David Heavener
·*The Vanishing Hitchhiker* (2020) Short Directed by Rosario Brucato
·*Amusement* (2008) Directed by John Simpson
·*The Backseat* (2009) Short Directed by Chris R. Notarile
·*When a Stranger Calls* (1979) Directed by Fred Walton
·*When a Stranger Calls* (2006) Directed by Simon West
·*The Sitter* (1977) Short Directed by Fred Walton
·*To Catch a Killer* (1992) Directed by Eric Till
·*Gacy* (2003) Directed by Clive Saunders
·*Voices in the Tunnels* (2008) Directed by Vic David
·*Dark Days* (2000) Directed by Marc Singer
·*Tales from the QuadeaD Zone* (1987) Directed by Chester Novell Turner
·*I Still Know What You Did Last Summer* (1998) Directed by Danny Cannon
·*Shtriga* (2019) Short Directed by Jayde Anderson